Podcasting for

Beginners

TABLE OF CONTENTS

CHAPTER ONE

SAY HELLO TO PODCASTING

Digital broadcasts have been readily available for the most recent decade. We hear them out while cooking, working out, driving, or cleaning the house and do whatever it takes not to pass up the scenes of the most loved ones. In the US just, 144 million individuals have sooner or later turned into a webcast which is practically 50% of the nation's populace. Presently would you be able to envision what number of individuals are tuning in to web recordings everywhere in the world?

The numbers should be amazing but at the same time what's great is the way that the local area of digital recording audience members has developed every year. Why are digital recordings so famous? What makes them popular on the planet in which visual students win? Remembering these inquiries and tuning in to the new arrangement of our most loved digital broadcasts out of sight, we can't resist the urge to discover answers by taking a gander at their past, present, and future.

A brief history of podcasting

Wikipedia says that the historical backdrop of podcasting follows back to the 1980s. Around then, it was known as sound publishing content to a blog. Nonetheless, the historical backdrop of current podcasting began quite recently, specifically, toward the start of the 2000s. With the arrival of the primary iPod in 2001, it got well known to transfer sound records to compact sound gadgets or connect them to RSS channels.

Two or after three years, when sound publishing content to a blog ended up being more open for the two audience members and substance makers than at any other time, Ben Hamersley, a writer at The Guardian instituted a "podcast". In his component for the media called "Perceptible unrest", he essentially joined two words – "iPod" and "broadcast" – together and concocted the term we as a whole use these days. The columnist likewise recommended to name it "Guerilla media" yet the thought didn't get on.

What is podcasting?

"Pod" – a versatile playback gadget, for example, an iPod or a portable playback gadget, for example, an iPod or some other MP3 player (a PC or PC some other MP3 player (a PC or personal computer likewise works). "Projecting" – got from broadcasting.

Podcasting is the dissemination of sight and sound records, for example, sound and video, over the Internet for playback on as sound and video, over the Internet for playback on cell phones or potentially PCs. RSS Most web recordings are shared (partnered) utilizing the RSS design - Real Simple Syndication. How is a digital recording not the same as a regular sound document? The key contrast is the appropriation model. Through RSS, anybody can buy into and "get" digital recordings, which can't avoid being which will be naturally podcast, consequently downloaded and oversaw by a downloaded and oversaw by a "case getting" program like iTunes. Straightforward sound documents should be found and downloaded physically by clients. What sorts of digital recordings would I be able to make? Talks for understudies to tune in to at their relaxation materials.

Planning Your Podcast:

There are two unavoidable issues you need to ask yourself here, and they're joined at the hip.

What's Your Podcast For?

So right off the bat, for what reason would you like to make a web recording? It is safe to say that you are a specialist? A business? Or then again an advertising chief? Assuming this is the case, you may have distinguished podcasting as an extraordinary method to assemble authority and furnish your clients and target crowd with significant and engaging substance. Or on the other hand, would you say you are taking a gander at podcasting from a specialist viewpoint? This may mean you'll make a show in your extra time. Furthermore, the subject will be something that you're enthusiastic about. In one or the other case, you can distinguish your "why" here. That is imperative to remember, so you can remain propelled, in any event, when you're thinking that it's hard to get a show out. Next, shouldn't something be said about your "who"?

Who is Your Podcast For?

So the first day, get the central issue in: Who are you causing this to digital broadcast for? The thing is, except if you know precisely who you're making your show for, and why you're doing it, you have zero chance of growing a crowd of people. In case you're coming at it from a business perspective, and you're (for instance) a fitness coach who needs to make a wellbeing and wellness digital recording, at that point, your intended interest group may be individuals who are keen on good dieting, weight reduction, exercise, or working out. In case you're making a side interest show – suppose it's based around your adoration for zombies and dystopian fiction – at that point, your intended interest group would just be people with similar energy. They may be aficionados of TV shows like The Walking Dead, computer games like Resident Evil, books like World War Z, and movies like Night of the Living Dead.

Who is your digital recording for?

A lot of keen individuals talk about making the audience personas or symbols. It's a smart thought, outlining out precisely who it is that you'd prefer to tune in to your substance. That persona is something to remember each time you plan a scene: "Would John, our audience persona, similar to this? Is this centered on what he loves, what he's keen on?" That persona and those inquiries assist you with keeping your show zeroed in and on target, the two of which make for an additionally captivating substance. So once you know who you need to reach, how would you contact them? You need to give individuals motivation to tune in. This implies making content that they will get something out of when they hit play. We'll discuss that just quickly, however first up, here are a few assets for you to bookmark for future perusing.

WHAT'S WITH THE PODCAST CRAZE?

Digital recordings are blasting because they can be easy to deliver while likewise a decent method to assemble a reliable finishing a special configuration for recounting your story, as per Beth Brodsky, leader of Iris Creative. She introduced tips on the best way to record and deal with a digital broadcast during the meeting "Making, Managing and Marketing a Podcast" (#19NTCpodcast) at the current year's Nonprofit Technology Conference (NTC) in Portland, Ore.

She introduced a few insights about exactly how famous digital recordings have become. The greater part of the U.S. populace has tuned in to a digital recording. Practically 50% of webcast listening is done at home and 22 percent is done in the vehicle. Also, web recording audience members are steadfast, wealthy, and instructed. Four out of five tunes in to all or the vast majority of each digital recording scene and tunes in to a normal of seven shows for every week.

Digital recordings don't need major speculation. They can be created using the PC in your office if you have the correct gear, which doesn't need to be an enormous cost. You'll require a PC, mouthpiece, earphones, recording programming, and facilitating administration.

Why are podcasts so popular now?

- Podcasts consider performing various tasks.
- Listening to a web recording is a simple method to make up for lost time with the most recent news and occasions.
- Podcasts are engaging.
- Podcast variations will fill in numbers.
- Smart speakers will push the limits of podcasting.

HOW ARE PODCASTS MADE?

Podcasts are made from the following steps:

A: Planning Your Podcast

B: Planning Your Episodes

C: Recording Your Podcast

D: Editing & Producing Your Podcast

E: Publishing Your Podcast

A: Planning Your Podcast:-

Stage 1:-

• Choosing a subject and name

• Show and scene design

• Cover craftsmanship creation

- Intro and outro music

- Equipment choice

- Audio recording and altering

- Submission to Apple Podcasts (iTunes)

- Advertise your digital recording

- Podcasting is a significantly less swarmed and serious space than writing for a blog, making now the ideal opportunity to begin.

- As of January 2021, there are simply over 1.75 million digital broadcasts, however, more than 600 million web journals.

Stage 2:-

Arranging:

This is the underlying (regularly disregarded) stage to make a digital recording. You'll need to invest a decent measure of energy here before you proceed onward. Don't hesitate to get out a scratch pad or a whiteboard so you can begin arranging your digital broadcast like a star.

Pick a Topic

You need your webcast to be centered on a specific theme. Attempt to limit it down to something you can talk about for some scenes (100+) however that isn't expansive to the point that you won't interest your possible crowd. For instance, rather than having an "open-air" digital broadcast, talk about investigating like investigating food, investigating territories, climbing – or considerably more explicit, such as climbing 14ers. You can generally extend your subject later as you get more mainstream. A significant point is that see the part about picking a name to ensure you don't restrict yourself.

Pick a Co-host (discretionary)

Do you have a companion, colleague, or associate that you need to co-have with? It very well may be a lot simpler to begin podcasting on the off chance that you have a co-have. You will normally have an all the more captivating discussion on the off chance that you both offer your perspectives on a point. It can likewise be useful to have somebody to keep things on target. Besides, you can part extra assignments of altering, advancing, and that's only the tip of the iceberg. There can be drawbacks, however. You'll need to ensure both of you focused on it as long as possible. What's more, it assists with setting a timetable from the earliest starting point so you know when you will record each week. There aren't governs here, however. If your co-have drops off, you could at present proceed with the digital recording without them. Or then again you could begin solo and add a co-have later. The significant thing is to simply begin. So how about we pick a name:

Pick a Name

There are three principle camps with regards to naming your show.

Choice 1 – The Clever Name

You may think about a truly shrewd name for your show. In any case, recollect that individuals should have the option to discover it when they're looking for data about your subject. If you have a smart/appealing name for your show, at that point attempt to likewise fuse a portrayal into the title. There's no point putting out incredible substance if no one can discover it. For instance, one of our shows is called the Path of Most Resistance. It presumably falls into the 'smart name' class, although we're not excessively shrewd... So, to give a touch of depiction, we likewise utilize the slogan: The Uncommon Leader's Guide.

Choice 2 – The Descriptive Name

The accessible (however some may state exhausting) decision is to just call your show what your intended interest group is looking for.

On the off chance that our fitness coach considered her show The Fitness Podcast, at that point there's positively no uncertainty regarding what is the issue here. It's a smart thought, albeit conceivably diminishes how paramount it is, a tad. Try not to get excessively long and tedious on the off chance that you go down this course. Recall that you'll have to state the digital broadcast name a considerable amount when recording your scenes, so ensure it moves off the tongue.

Choice 3 – Using Your Name

This is essentially a no-no except if you've just got a crowd of people. If somebody began 'The Mike Smith Show' and it was about stone climbing, individuals would simply think "who is Mike Smith?" and proceed onward to the following digital recording. Once more, you can consolidate this into your show's name alongside something unmistakable ('Rock Climbing, with Mike Smith'). In any case, try not to name the show after you with no different subtleties.

Picking a Podcast Format

The arrangement you pick is truly close to home, and relies upon who's included! If it's simply you, you're not doing a co-facilitated show any time soon, for instance. The thing is, it's comparative here to your web recording length: while it's acceptable to have a 'normal' design, so your audience members realize what's in store, you don't need to adhere to it without fail. You may be alright with a specific arrangement and subside into a section, or you may incline toward a 'mishmash' approach. It's absolutely up to you. So what are the normal kinds of web recording show designs?

The Solo Show

Otherwise called the talk. Advantages: You don't have to depend on any other individual to record your scenes, and you're fabricating a standing as the expert regarding your matter. The web recording is likewise only yours, so you can settle on decisions on sponsorship and adaptation. Also, you don't have to part the benefits with anybody. Difficulties: Perhaps the scariest style of show for the tenderfoot podcaster. Perhaps the greatest test of the performance show is getting over the inclination that you're 'conversing with yourself' and understanding that you're conversing with the audience.

The Co-Hosted Show

Introducing close by a companion or partner.

Advantages: An incredible route around the 'mic dismay' or recording alone is to visit on the show with another person. On the off chance that you locate the correct co-have, you have somebody to skip off, banter, or even false (don't be excessively mean!). Some co-facilitated web recordings have incredible science between the moderators. This can make a five-star listening experience. Difficulties: Not just do you need to put aside an ideal opportunity to record, yet that time should likewise be appropriate for your co-have. There's likewise the topic of possession: whose webcast right? Do you split any future pay 50/50? What's more, what occurs if your co-have loses interest or gets inaccessible later on?

The Interview Show

'Getting' the aptitude or diversion estimation of others.

Advantages: Talking to your legends. Doing a meeting show offers you the chance to sit down to talk with somebody you've generally turned upward to. On top of this, your visitors will have their crowds who may tune in to the meeting and wind up buying into your show. Whenever done right, you can truly grow a group of people thusly.

Difficulties: Interviewing is an expertise that you'll have to sharpen through training, so don't move toward the A listens in your field straight away. You'll have to continually discover and move toward expected visitors, plan meets, and depend on others to appear (face to face or carefully). You additionally need to depend on innovation to work appropriately all through each call.

Different Formats

At long last, there are a lot of different arrangements that aren't so normally utilized, however may well suit you. For instance, you have:

Roundtable – One customary host and various visitors, talking through one explicit point (e.g. The Game Design Roundtable).

Narrative – A storyteller strolls you through a scope of meetings, discussions, and on the spot, clasps to paint an image (e.g. Startup)

Documentary -Drama – A blend of dramatization and narrative. Offering learning and information, however in an engaging way (e.g. threatening Worlds).

On the off chance that you need more assistance, we have a full manual for designs, including their stars, cons, and how to go about it, inside the dispatch course inside the Podcast Host Academy. All upheld by our week by week live Q&A meetings.

B: Planning Your Episodes

In the wake of building up what sort of substance you'd prefer to put out in your digital recording, it's an ideal opportunity to consider the scenes themselves. In this way, when seeing how to begin a webcast, what are the absolute most normal inquiries regarding digital recording scenes

How Long Should A Podcast Episode Be?

Digital recording length relies entirely upon content. Try not to chop down great substance or cushion out compact work! How long does it should be to get the message out? On the off chance that you asked most web recording audience members, a "short" scene would presumably be anything under 15 minutes. What's more, a "long" scene would most likely be anything longer than 60 minutes.

How long sought a digital broadcast be straightforward?

Many will reference the hour of the normal drive (said to associate with 20 minutes) as a decent length to go for. In any case, anything from 20 as long as 45 minutes is by all accounts inside the "sweet spot" for a scene length. Try not to stress a lot over these figures however, at last, your scene lengths ought to be chosen by two things.

· Your substance

Your crowd

If you have 50 minutes of significant, important substance, why cleave it down to 20? Or on the other hand similarly, if you've said all that you need to state shortly, why cushion it out to 30? In extraordinary cases, state you do a meeting and it's an incredible discussion beginning to end yet runs for 2 hours. You can generally hack it down the middle and make two scenes. Over the long haul, your audience members will advise you if they think your scenes are excessively short or excessively long. Attempt to review your crowd once every year to accumulate information like this, and you can change likewise.

At the point when you get that information, there's no compelling reason to adhere to a similar length each time, however, it's acceptable to have a 'normal' so your audience members realize what's in store. At long last, length can be an 'interesting' factor, similar to what we discussed in Section 3. Short and smart brief scenes could suit a specific sort of audience, or a tremendous 3 hour top to bottom meetings may suit another. Consider whether length may be a conscious special decision for you.

How Often Should I Release New Episodes?

This is one of the greatest starter questions. Here's the appropriate response: The best timetable is typically the most continuous one that you can adhere to, consistently. Thus, if you can just oversee once every month, that is fine. On the off chance that you can deal with like clockwork, stunningly better. On the off chance that you can oversee week by week, at that point that is incredible.

17

You can in any case have a major contact with fortnightly, or month to month shows, yet individuals plan their lives around what day of the week it is. It's the daily schedule at the front line of our lives, and taking advantage of it tends to be amazing. All things considered, adhering to a cutoff time only for it is trivial. You'll have a greater effect if you put out one amazing scene a month rather than an extremely normal scene consistently.

Another Option:

Podcasting in seasons

Season podcasting gets you off the distributing treadmill, bringing the fun back into podcasting! Beginning a digital recording doesn't need to resemble hopping on a treadmill, where you need to get another scene out each week/fortnight/month. You can follow some guidelines from TV's experience and web recording in seasons. At the point when you start an occasional webcast, each season will normally have a subject. You may make scenes based around that subject or point for 6-12 scenes, at that point have a break. Following a month or two, you'll dispatch another season (with another topic/theme) and rehash the cycle. An illustration of an occasional webcast is our special Podcast, where season 1 (refreshed on season 10) was tied in with being a tenderfoot podcaster. Next, season 2 was tied in with podcasting gear, season 3 was tied in with building a web recording site, etc.

If your substance is fitting for it, you can even transform each season into a course or a digital book sometime later, so there are numerous advantages to occasional podcasting. One trap, in any case, is that you may lose force (and the interest of your crowd) during your breaks. We've found, however, that on the off chance that you set them up for it, and clarify when you'll be back, at that point you battle the two issues. You can't miss your own cutoff time all things considered!

C: Recording Your Podcast

Recording Equipment

The absolute minimum you need to record a digital broadcast is a PC with a USB amplifier and admittance to the web. When in doubt, however, the more restricted and cheaper your arrangement and gear, the more restricted the sound nature of your show will be. Straightforward USB amplifier arrangements can give great outcomes if you pick the privilege mic. Also, you are vastly improved to begin and see whether you appreciate it before working out huge amounts of cash on sound gear. Given that, the Samson Q2U is our top pick for a quality and reasonable mic. It could last you years, and you can utilize it with a wide range of other chronicle hardware, as well. Accessibility relies upon where you are on the planet, however, the ATR2100 is a practically indistinguishable choice. Neither should interfere with you more than $100!

The Samson accompanies a little mic stand, yet a decent update is a blast arm mic remain, to give you a touch greater adaptability. There's an advantage to keeping things basic in that it's anything but difficult to record. That implies you'll have the option to keep the show normal in the good 'of days and truly allow yourself to assemble a dependable after. In case you're wanting to do a ton of in-person meets, the Rode Startled+ is an incredible instrument. Two of them, in addition to the SC6 splitter, make for a truly light, straightforward meeting arrangement. From that point, you can move up to a stunningly better USB mic (like the Rode Podcaster), or perhaps overhaul your arrangement with the Zoom Pod Track P4. The P4 is a pristine digital broadcast recorder that allows you to record 4 members locally, just as far off visitors. It's an awesome all-rounder bit of digital broadcast gear. Peruse our survey of the Zoom Pod Track P4 to get the full lowdown. In case you're searching for more data on gear, here's elite, to begin with:

· Best webcast receivers

· Best USB receivers

· Best advanced recorders

Keep in mind, we have a starter gear direct inside our Podcast Launch course, and we additionally have various separate top to bottom Podcast Equipment courses, if that is all you require. Besides, we love to talk gear, so go along with us in one of our weeks by week individuals just Q&As, to get some information about sparkly things.

Recording and Editing Software

At the point when you plug your USB mouthpiece into your PC, you will require some product to record and alter the sound. Fortunately, there's a couple of alternatives for this, and one of them doesn't cost you anything.

Boldness: a decent quality, for nothing pocket sound altering application. For most individuals, it takes into account all your podcasting requirements.

Adobe Audition: my #1 Pro-level creation instrument – the steep expectation to absorb information, yet extraordinary work process, and highlight rich. It's accessible through a paid membership. Look at Adobe Audition VS Audacity.

Alito: The Podcast Maker: the most straightforward conceivable experience. This is a web application that can computerize sound cleanup, adding music, and distributing it to your host. It additionally offers extraordinary altering and scene-building instruments.

In The Podcast Host Academy, we have a course that shows you how to utilize Audacity for cleanup, altering, and creation. Look at Audacity Podcast Production for full subtleties. On the off chance that you go to the 'Web recording Maker' course, or simply need to perceive how it functions, look at our guide on the best way to make a digital broadcast with Alito. In case you are a Mac client, you will most likely have a Garage band introduced naturally on your machine. That is famous sound programming with podcasters as well, albeit late forms have truly chopped down the highlights it offers.

Nowadays, I would suggest even Mac clients getting hold of Audacity as a free other option.

D: Editing & Producing Your Podcast

Next stop, creation! This is the place where you alter out mix-ups, fasten together extraordinary brief snippets, include music or FX, and ensure it's all sounding incredible with EQ, leveling, pressure and the sky is the limit from there.

Altering your Podcast

In this way, you may now be recording with Audacity. Provided that this is true, this is likewise a decent stage for creation. We have an extensive video course inside The Podcast Host Academy intended to divert you from complete apprentice to dominate maker. Furthermore, you can ask us all your consuming altering inquiries in our week after week lives Q&A uphold meetings, for individuals as it were. Look at it to begin. If you need a starter direct on what kind of altering to do, look at our article on the MEE Podcast Production measure. This keeps altering straightforward and reliable.

Get Someone Else to Edit Your Show?

In case you're set up to go through a touch of cash to save time however, you can generally reevaluate your altering and recruit another person to do it for you. You'll discover alternatives for all spending plans and necessities over at our Podcast Production Directory.

The Simplest Option – Alito: The Podcast Maker Consider the possibility that you've never utilized altering programming. Perhaps you're worried that you don't have the spending plan to rethink your creation, yet also, don't have the opportunity to learn it all. On the off chance that that is the situation, you should look at Alito, the 'digital recording making' apparatus, which constructs your scene for you. All are truly easy to utilize. You can record your scenes directly into it, and it'll deal with the handling, altering, and distributing of your webcast, without the requirement for any genuine altering programming. It's likewise got a library of music and jingles now that by-pass any need to locate your sound marking (see beneath!).

So whether you're a finished amateur, or an accomplished podcaster looking to radically eliminate your creation time: The Podcast Maker could be the appropriate response you're searching for!

Music for your Podcast

There's no standard to state your webcast should have music, yet many decide to add some toward the start and end to add that additional layer of polished skill. Even though you may see movies or TV shows with 1 moment + of introduction music, do not duplicate this in your digital recording. I would state that you would prefer not to have a bit of music all alone for any more than 15 seconds.

E: Publishing Your Podcast

At last, how to get your web recording on the web and out to the world!

Cover Art

Much the same as your scene titles, early introductions are everything. Having alluring cover craftsmanship that stands apart is essential when your show lines facing a huge number of others in the Apple/iTunes store.

Much the same as music, imaginative hall authorizing can be found in visual workmanship as well. Numerous podcasters utilize imaginative house/stock pictures to make cover workmanship on stages like Canova.

You can likewise have fine art handcrafted by a consultant. On the other hand, you can approach a creative or photography-cherishing companion to check whether they will help you set up something.

Preferably, your cover craftsmanship ought to be 1400 x 1400 pixels, in JPG or PNG structure, and under 500kb in size. Adhere to these specs and it'll assist you with trying not to have any issues in catalogs like Apple/iTunes. Your craftsmanship will regularly be seen by possible audience members in a lot more modest arrangement, so try not to mess it brimming with subtleties that could transform it into a wreck. It ought to be unmistakably intelligible when just around 200px wide.

Picking Your Podcast Hosting

With regards to getting your webcast out there for everybody to hear, you'll need a web recording facilitating account, in some cases called a media to have. Media or podcasts has are administrations that store your sound and permit your audience members to tune in, download, and buy into your web recording. One normal misguided judgment when figuring out how to make a digital recording is that you transfer your webcast to places like iTunes. This isn't the situation. As this was a now and again posed inquiry, we discussed media has and getting your show into Apple/iTunes in detail in our 'How to Upload a Podcast' article. To put it, however, you need to join with a media facilitating administration to have your sound records, and you can either have a site set up on their webpage to convey them or spot them on your current site.

We utilize a couple of various media hosts, and you can peruse our opinion about them all here:

The Best Podcast Hosting Services or on the other hand, here are what I see as the best 3 hosts available at this moment, and the contrasts between:

Buzz sprout is the least expensive top choice, and generally well known ($12/month)

Charm has incredible development and private digital broadcast highlights ($19/month)

Semiconductor likewise offers private webcast takes care of and is very basic ($19/month)

Submitting to Directories

Whenever you've made your show inside your media host of decision, you would then be able to submit it to different indexes, where audience members can find, buy in to, and download it.

Any great host – and every one of the three I've recorded above – will have a fair arrangement of auto-submit or guided-accommodation instruments. Thus, they make it simple to get your show into Apple Podcasts, Sportily, Google Podcasts, and other well-known spots.

CHAPTER TWO

WHY SHOULD YOU START ONE?

How to Use Podcasting to Improve Your Business

For those of you who don't have a clue what a web recording is, it is a progression of advanced sound or video documents that a client can download and tune in to. As per Podcast Insights, 51% of the US populace has tuned in to a webcast. Since 2013 there has been a consistent 20% expansion in webcast tuning in. These days everybody from your neighborhood business visionary to your companions from secondary school is beginning a web recording. As you read further, you will figure out how podcasting can improve your image just as the stuff to make a digital recording fruitful.

How Could Podcasting Improve Your Brand?

- It will contact new crowds having your webcast accessible on all stages will permit you to contact crowds that are not previously following your online media destinations. When audience members buy into a sound arrangement, they are bound to hold tuning into your web recording as long as you keep on creating great scenes. Your crowd is likewise bound to prescribe your show to different audience members.
- It can construct enduring associations with audience members over time, audience members will feel a feeling of association with your show and the hosts. This will construct trust with the audience members and urges them to interface with your image.

- It's connecting with the audience among the everyday hurrying around of bustling life, digital recordings offer their audience members a reprieve from the adequate measure of composed substance they see for the day. This offers the speaker the chance to pass on their message in a profoundly intelligent manner.
- It's an extraordinary expansion to your showcasing Promoting your web recording all through your online media and blog entries can give you new and new substance to advance outside of your other substance advertising. Cross-advancing will likewise acquire you, new devotees, on the entirety of your social stages notwithstanding adding audience members/endorsers of your digital recording arrangement. Since we tended to how podcasting can improve your image, here are a few hints on the stuff to make a web recording effective:
- Establish a subject you need to give your crowd an overall thought of what is the issue here, and you can do this effectively by building up a topic. This will better limit your objective audience.
- Create a name–Your web recording ought to have a snappy name that goes with the subject of the show. Although having your organization name as the title of your show is right, this will allow you to get inventive and think outside about the crate!
- Design a logo–Having a logo for your show will separate you from other web recordings and make it simpler for your crowd to discover you.
- Include an expert presentation (with music) – This ought to be in an expert voice, much like the introduction to a public broadcast. It ought to incorporate a short portrayal of what be the issue here and a source of inspiration that keeps the audience needing more.
- Choose the correct visitors If you decide to have various visitors on your show, you need to ensure they work out in a

good way for the subject of your digital broadcast. A special reward with having a visitor on your show is they can impart your scene to their adherents and you could acquire endorsers.

- Edit your scenes appropriately you need to ensure each scene is altered expertly. If an audience tunes into your scene and there are altering mistakes, it could stop them from proceeding to tune in to that scene or buying into your digital recording.

Podcasting Brings Increased Web Traffic:

"Consistently I'm getting messages from individuals who are disclosing to me they discovered me through the digital broadcast," said Flynn, who noticed that he saw an expansion in site traffic when he began to webcast. "It's difficult to completely tell [the traffic came from the podcast] since its sound so individuals can't click a connection," he said. Be that as it may, Flynn is positive the digital recording is the main consideration in his expanded rush hour gridlock. A month in the wake of the beginning, he presented a report on the blog demonstrating some early outcomes

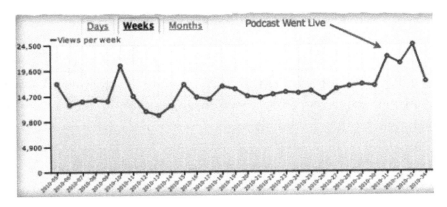

Flynn saw increased website traffic immediately after he started podcasting. Barely a year later, had he posted an overview on his blog asking individuals how they initially discovered him? He was overwhelmed by the outcomes. The biggest level of blog peruses had discovered him through his digital broadcast. The True Power of

Podcasting Flynn feels so emphatically about the force of podcasting that he built up a podcasting instructional exercise to help other people gain from his experience.

"Podcasting has assisted me with improving as a communicator," said Flynn. "Getting behind the amplifier has assisted me with imparting my crowd and in actuality." Exceptional Note: If in the wake of perusing this post you choose to begin podcasting, I'd emphatically propose you look at my companions at Podcast Websites. They're the ONLY people I prescribe with regards to all you require to make, develop and adapt your webcast – including the real facilitating of your digital broadcast, as well... their 24-hour client assistance is remarkable, as well. Lovely people of the jury, I remain before you today given one objective. I will exhibit without question, why your crowd WANTS, however, NEEDS you to consider beginning a digital broadcast. Yet, before we address the reasons why your business needs a voice, how about we start by defying the three reasons why individuals commonly evade it and why, if you've been doing moreover, they should at this point don't hold you up.

Evasion REASON #1: I Don't Have an Audience

I thoroughly get it. Why start a web recording, if there's no crowd to make it for, isn't that so? This is quite possibly the most well-known complaints about beginning a web recording, yet the incongruity is that a webcast is an incredible method to start BUILDING a group of people. The rising ubiquity of web recordings joined with the way that they're handily devoured (in contrast to perusing a long article, or digital book) implies you'll have a far more prominent possibility of building an unwavering crowd that preferences, trusts and feels like they know you.

Shirking REASON #2: I Don't Have Room in My House/Business for a Studio

On the off chance that you have a work area – you have all the room you require for a digital recording. This is the place where I digital broadcast: Since podcasting is still generally new, our brain will in general connection the idea of podcasting – to radio telecom. Yet, that couldn't possibly be more off-base. A portion of the present most famous web recordings is being made in a little corner of a room. Furthermore, you needn't bother with that extravagant amplifier to begin, all things considered. Trust me. I just utilized my Apple earphones when I began in 2010.

Evasion REASON #3: I Can't Afford the Equipment

You'll be astonished by how little you need to start.

All you required is…

• Computer.

• Microphone.

• Podcasting Software (Mac accompanies Garage band previously incorporated into its applications).

• A great subject to examine.

10 Reasons Why Your Business Needs a Voice!

#1 People super like digital broadcasts these days

As per the late examination directed by Edison, Research podcasting keeps on indicating solid development in recent years. Truth be told, many accept that 2017 will be the break-out year for business podcasting, especially.

#2 Not every person has the opportunity to peruse 4550 words

The normal blog entries are around 700-words, which can be perused in around 5-minutes. What could be compared to 6.5 blog entries? In addition to the fact that this allows you to convey more substance to your crowd, but at the same time it's conveyed such that's anything but difficult to burn-through. What's more, as a side note, in case you're not exploiting tuning in to digital broadcasts during your drive to and from your work environment, or while going for a stroll, or on a plane excursion, you're passing up a gigantic chance to use your time.

#3 it's simpler to deliver a steady digital recording, than blog entries

"On the off chance that you need to be an essayist, you should complete two things over all others: read a great deal and compose a ton. It is extremely unlikely around these two things that I'm mindful of, no alternate route." — Stephen King

Hold up! If the incomparable Stephen King is stating there's no alternate way to composing, at that point I don't get that's meaning for most of us? The uplifting news anyway is that podcasting permits you to make an astounding bit of substance without experiencing endless updates of your work. Truth be told, the more conversational and easygoing it is, the better it will associate with your crowd. That is probably the greatest commendation I get about my digital broadcast, you pruner FM – which it resembles several companions talking in a bar, or over supper. Be that as it may, if you'd, in any case, prefer to tidy up your sound in the wake of recording you can without much of a stretch locate a cheap editorial manager on up work and have them take out any stops or "us" and "eras".

#4 Podcasts are tacky

At the point when somebody chooses to tune in to a web recording they'll typically tune in to the whole show, and on the off chance that they like it, there's a decent possibility they may tune in to another. That is a LOT of substance! What's extraordinary about this is that they'll either feel nearer or reverberate with your message, or they'll conclude this isn't the perfect spot for them, and that is something worth being thankful for. The general purpose of getting your voice out there is to draw in and assemble the correct crowd for YOU and your business.

#5 Your image will profit

I'm a gigantic adherent to building an individual brand, yet having a noteworthy logo and infectious trademark will just qualify you as being normal in the present advanced commercial center. What's most significant is that your business has a character. Also, I can think about no better method to give your business a character than by giving it your VOICE!

#6 Become a moment, invited visitor

At the point when somebody tunes in to your digital recording, you've unexpectedly gotten the "welcomed visitor" inside their home or office. The same as sitting opposite this audience and having an eye to eye meeting with their full focus. No doubt! That is amazing stuff. Try not to misunderstand me. I'm a colossal aficionado of email advertising, video promoting, and reliable substance showcasing, (for example, blog entries and infographics), yet there's nothing similar to the degree of closeness podcasting makes.

#7 Align yourself with fruitful individuals

If you decide to dispatch and grow a meeting design webcast, each one of those visitors you'll be pursuing down to have gone ahead of your show will affect your general image, as well. The more fruitful individuals you have on your show from your industry, or specialty, the closer adjusted you'll be seen to them and their prosperity. Insight is critical and is regularly extremely, infectious.

#8 The on-going overhauling of your current crowd

Regardless of how huge or little your present crowd I can ensure they're tuning in to digital broadcasts. So if they're leaving they approach to open your messages, read your blog entries, and register for your online courses – why not help them with a digital broadcast! Not exclusively will your webcast help structure a more profound relationship, however, it can likewise fill in as a stage to highlight individuals from your crowd who are incorporating your educating. Some all the content you can make are contextual analyses, which show that what you educate works. My amigo Pat Flynn does this well than nearly every other person I know.

#9 Develop your talking aptitudes

I love talking, however like whatever else, talking is an ability that should be created. Great about podcasting that it will permit you to consistently deal with your art. It additionally causes you to construct trust in your talking capacity without requiring the endorsing chuckling, or praise from a live crowd. It very well may be somewhat bizarre addressing an imperceptible crowd, however, that equivalent ability will assist you with conveying drawing in and engaging online classes, which is expertise each advanced business visionary ought to be improving.

#10 Opportunity to repurpose content

Each of your digital broadcast scenes can be repurposed into extra bits of substance.

Here's a couple of thoughts:

- Have your webcast translated and refined into a solitary blog entry with a source of inspiration for tuning in to the whole show.

- Have the best purposes of your digital recording transformed into a 7-point, or 10-point infographic.
- Breakup a solitary webcast recording into 2 or 3 scenes. I energetically suggest this if you have the chance to pull in a famous visitor to your show. Simply make a point to convey ahead of time to them that you plan on separating it into 2 or 3 shows that way you two can appropriately arrange for what to cover and where to split things up.
- Turn a portion of your most downloaded webcast scenes into Slide decks to share utilizing social, or even into live introductions.
- The openings for repurposing are in a real sense perpetual.

Podcast Advertising: What You Need To Know:

What number of digital recordings are there? As indicated by Apple insights, there are 525,000 dynamic webcast shows with more than 18.5 million scenes.

The extent of Americans tuning in to digital recordings has almost multiplied in the previous nine years and is projected to keep developing for a long time to come. Also, since interest in podcasting has risen so strongly, an expanding number of publicists are utilizing this pattern to advance their items and administrations. As per the Podcasting Audit Study by Bridge Ratings, promoters are relied upon to burn through $500 million on web recording advertisements in 2021 – a pattern that goes ahead the impact points of critical past development in the area.

How could promoters influence podcasting to get the most elevated potential ROI? There are two vital components to progress:

- Create a connection with a digital recording that bolsters your image
- Develop a practical showcasing technique to assemble a crowd of people

Making a heavenly digital broadcast isn't simple, however, discovering approaches to advance it very well may be significantly more muddled. Luckily, there are various ways that you can spread the news. This is what you need to think about webcast promoting and how to showcase a web recording.

The extent of Americans tuning in to digital recordings has almost multiplied in the previous nine years and is projected to keep developing for a long time to come. What's more, since interest in podcasting has risen so pointedly, an expanding number of publicists are utilizing this pattern to advance their items and administrations. As indicated by the Podcasting Audit Study by Bridge Ratings, promoters are required to burn through $500 million on digital broadcast advertisements in 2021 – a pattern that goes ahead the impact points of critical past development in the area.

How might promoters influence podcasting to get the most noteworthy potential ROI? There are two pivotal components to progress:

- Create a drawing in a digital broadcast that bolsters your image
- Develop a financially savvy showcasing system to assemble a crowd of people

Making a heavenly digital recording isn't simple, however discovering approaches to advance it tends to be significantly more muddled. Luckily, there are various ways that you can spread the news. This is what you need to think about webcast publicizing and how to showcase a digital broadcast.

Related Content: How We Built the Growth Everywhere Podcast to 109,000 Listens every Month. Industry Standards for Podcast Sponsorship. There are two sorts of digital broadcast promotions that publicists can run: 1) the 15-second pre-roll and 2) the 60-second mid-roll.

Consider the digital broadcasts you often tune in to. Ordinarily, the digital broadcast host will discuss their patrons in one of two spots in the web recording — the start of the webcast, or the center of the web recording. Pre-move promotions are ordinarily around 15-seconds in length and are put before the "meat" of the show's substance. Before the host plunges into the digital recording content, they'll talk about the publicist's item or administration. Mid-move advertisements are put around the center of the show, typically after the audience has completed the process of tuning in to around 40-70% of the show's substance. Around the midway imprint, the host will discuss the publicist's substance. Some web recording has offer finish-of-show advertisements also. These normally function admirably, because they're the last advertisement that audience members hear before the show closes. It's the last source of inspiration as it were, which helps drive more outcomes for publicists. Ballpark Pricing for Podcast Advertising. As indicated by John Lee Dumas, digital broadcast publicizing rates that hosts charge are normally:

- $18 per 1,000 tunes in (CPMs) briefly pre-move promotion
- $25 per 1,000 tunes in (CPMs) briefly mid-move promotion

The almost certain audience members are to be effectively tuning in to an advertisement, the more it'll cost. The benefit of pre-move promotions may be lower cost, however, you may get the same number of individuals tuning in to the advertisement given the way that they haven't gotten into the substance yet. Mid-move advertisements cost more, yet audience members are likely previously drawn in with the digital recording scene by then, so they cost more.

Understanding Your Audience

In case you're engaged with advertising, you should as of now have a definite comprehension of the socioeconomics that your image is focusing on. All things considered, you may not completely get why the clients you think you know all around are watching a digital broadcast—and you'll have to adjust your endeavors to their assumptions before you can redo your webcast advertisement to address their issues. To get a feeling of how you can more readily comprehend your crowd, it's useful to perceive how the fundamental webcast promoters were effective. In the early long periods of this medium, the vast majority of the individuals who listened were web engineers and innovation, business people. The best organizations that publicized through web recordings zeroed in on this segment and realized how to tweak their message to their particular necessities.

Components of a Successful Podcast Ad Campaign

When you've unmistakably characterized your intended interest group—just as gotten a handle on why they're tuning in to digital recordings—you can utilize this new medium to effectively become your base of webcast devotees. Truth be told, there are various systems you can use to spread the news and fabricate your crowd, including the accompanying:

Exploit Podcast Directories

On the off chance that you run your digital broadcast, there are various online indexes you ought to investigate presenting your show to. It's a smart thought to introduce your digital broadcast to at any rate a couple of them to widen your openness. Here are a few indexes worth investigating:

iTunes

Everyone knows about iTunes, as it makes up 75% of the worldwide advanced music market. In any case, while a few people traits the beginning of podcasting to Apple (however the medium owes its name to Apple's iPod gadget), this type of correspondence got its beginning as sound contributing to a blog as far back as the 1980s. All things considered, iTunes is as yet an incredible method to share webcasts. To get recorded, you'll need to experience an endorsement cycle, which regularly requires a long time. To build your odds of getting your web recording affirmed, follow the tips laid out on their webcast specs page, including the accompanying primary prerequisites:

- Viewers should have the option to get to the substance without entering a secret word.
- It should meet the RSS 2.0 determination.
- You ought to incorporate the suggested iTunes RSS labels.
- You should set the <explicit> tag to "yes" if you plan on utilizing any profane language in your web recording. Remember that you can't utilize express language in your title, portrayal, or cover craftsmanship, regardless of whether you utilize this tag.
- You can't utilize any pictures that praise sex, medications, viciousness, or other substances that might be deciphered as revolting.
- You are denied from utilizing reserved words or pictures without earlier approval from the brand name holders.
- However long your image isn't profoundly disputable, you shouldn't experience any difficulty getting your web recording distributed in the iTunes posting. Make certain to utilize fitting labels in the titles and portrayal because the iTunes web crawler utilizes these labels to help clients find applicable digital recordings, so it will build your odds of being found.

Pod nova

Case nova is another well-known assistance for making, facilitating, and posting digital broadcasts. Individuals from the administration can get to various extraordinary podcasting instruments, for example, VLC Media Player and Podcast Studio. Furthermore, since so many digital broadcast engineers utilize the stage to meet their specialized requirements, it's likewise an incredible discussion for individuals to discover other web recordings to follow. There are a huge number of digital broadcasts recorded on unit nova, so you should be shrewd to guarantee that your accommodation sticks out. Here are a few interesting points:

- Choose your classification shrewdly. Unit nova has 15 unique classes that you can look over. A portion of these classes have a lot a larger number of entries than others, so being recorded locally with fewer other web recordings will improve the probability of potential fans finding yours. For instance, there are around 10,000 digital broadcasts recorded in the "Organization" class, while just around 4,000 are recorded under "Security." If you're running a webcast on organization security issues, at that point your smartest option might be to submit to the security segment so you won't rival the same number of other digital broadcasts has for consideration.
- Update your digital recording profile reasonably routinely. As a matter of course, web recordings are shown by Pod nova as per their ubiquity. Be that as it may, clients have the choice of arranging them by the date they were last altered. On the off chance that you update your digital broadcast routinely, it'll be appeared at the first spot on these lists, altogether improving your probability of being found. Chances are, you won't get the same number of supporters from Pod nova as iTunes, yet it's as yet a decent spot to get some additional visits.

Unit Bean

Unit Bean is another extraordinary stage for both facilitating and advancing your webcasts. You can liberate up your web recordings for the administration, however, you can likewise pay extra for facilitating, custom pictures, and different highlights. As per Quant cast, this site gets about a large portion of 1,000,000 one of a kind guests a month, making it an incredible spot to produce a group of people.

Medrol

Medrol is an illustration of a promotion organization that centers on web recording publicizing. Medrol gives sponsors admittance to many shows that focus on the kind of crowd that they're searching for. They target has who incorporate promotions successfully into their show, with the goal that the advertisement seems as though it's locally positioned. Digital broadcasts can drive critical ROI for a business. For instance, digital recordings turned into the number 1 marketing.

CHAPTER THREE

BEFORE YOU START: BRAND ASSESSMENT

- 4 steps to successful marketing
- Exercise: defining your brand
- Steps to creating good content for your podcast

Over 90% of entrepreneurs accept that having an exceptional brand that separates them from the opposition is very important.1 Over a portion of them likewise reports marking as being basic to pulling in new business.2 What privileged insights do solid brands as Apple and Coke hold? What's more, how could entrepreneurs use them as a wellspring of motivation? Here are four stages to building an effective brand.

1. Characterize how you need to be seen

When your clients have wrapped up utilizing your item or administration, how would you need them to depict their experience? On the off chance that you own a café, for instance, what do you need them to state?

"Amazing, this café has the biggest bits around. It's incredible!"

"You truly feel like you've been welcomed for a customary Italian family supper. The dishes are basic however so scrumptious!"

"The assistance is snappy and the food is OK, however, the cost is phenomenal!"

Consider you're to be as your guarantee to your clients – a guarantee that is not quite the same as your rivals'.

2. Put together your business dependent on this guarantee

Keeping the guarantee that separates you from your rivals suggests that you're accomplishing something more than what they're doing. The café that needs to be perceived at its unparalleled costs, for instance, should figure out how to amplify the number of clients served per table in one night. The edge per singular client will be less, however, the number of clients will compensate for it. All in all, your image will incredibly impact the triumphant equation that you'll put together your business concerning.

3. Impart your guarantee

The entirety of your promoting material – from the shades of your logo to your site text – should be created as an element of this guarantee. What you state on Facebook or LinkedIn should be lined up with this message, as must the adornment of your premises. It's at this stage that your image gets key to your promoting efforts. Likewise, your advertisements will be considerably more compelling, since you'll have a reasonable message to pass on.

4. Be reliable

In the wake of characterizing how you need to be seen, at that point putting together your business dependent on this discernment and conveying this guarantee, you should be reliable. Apple, for instance, is perceived for making items that are both exquisite and imaginative: it can't stand to dispatch another ugly telephone or another tablet that is innovatively behind, because that would mean breaking the guarantee it has made to its clients. The thought here is to create trust.

Your clients should at this point don't consider you to be a guarantee however as a reality. Consistency is regularly the hardest part, yet the one with the best rewards. Over the long run, a very much oversaw brand quits turning into an organization guarantee and progressively turns into a client assumption. There might be 10 Italian cafés in the area, yet one in particular where clients hope to encounter a customary Italian family supper. That café's image is not, at this point its name or logo – it's the assumption for its clients. When applying such a methodology, your business will bit by bit have the option to increment the two its costs and its deals (believe it or not, both simultaneously!). Your image will get one of your business's most important resources and the one with the most effect on your primary concern.

Exercise: defining your brand

What is Brand Voice?

Brand voice alludes to the character and feeling imbued into an organization's correspondences. It incorporates everything from the words and language you use, to the character and pictures your promoting resources expect to conjure. It assumes a significant job in ensuring your message slices through the commotion and establishes a long term connection with likely clients.

Why is having a Strong Brand Voice Important?

The most suffering organizations have a solid character and away from the direction. Their message is conveyed reliably wherever they have a presence with a setup brand voice. Creating brand acknowledgment with shoppers requires consistency and redundancy. On the off chance that your character or informing seems to change habitually, it's harder for crowds to know precisely what you're about. Thus, your endeavors are probably going to crash and burn and miss out on a superior marked choice (regardless of whether they can coordinate your item quality).

What exactly is the Difference between Voice and Tone?

Notwithstanding your voice, it's likewise critical to get the tone.

Voice: This depicts your organization's character. It's reliable and constant.

Tone: The enthusiastic affectation applied to your voice. It changes with what's reasonable for a specific piece or message. While your voice stays steady, the tone may change as indicated by the setting of your informing. For instance, a web-based media post about a great deal would have a more carefree tone than one breaking news about an organization's emergency.

Investigating 3 Examples of Exceptional Brand Voices

On the off chance that this sounds conceptual and somewhat extreme to comprehend, that is alright. Now and again, it's simpler to see true guides to make an idea click. Thus, here are five brands that have nailed their voice.

Mail Chimp: Warm. Inviting. Supportive.

Email promoting can be confounded, however, Mail Chimp's voice strengthens their foundation's usability.

Take this model from their landing page: The feature improves the arrangement mail Chimp offers in a manner everybody can comprehend.

Duluth Trading Company: Irreverent. Definitive. Pragmatic.

Duluth Trading Company has practical experience in solid yet engaging apparel for working individuals. This is reflected in their marking, which utilizes sharp duplicate that clarifies the advantages of their items while standing apart with downplayed humor. This is clear when you visit their site. For instance, take their No Tug Tank Top. It's a tank top that is longer in the back, to abstain from waiting to be pulled down when hanging over (as one may do while planting).

CHAPTER FOUR

WHAT IS A PODCASTING

- What Kind of Media can make up a Podcast?
- What's the Difference between an Audio File and a Podcast Episode?
- Using Podcasts as a Listener

The ideal everything for webcasts

We get a significant kick out of learning the ideal length and recurrence for various sorts of substances, and podcasting is no special case. There's less examination out there about web recordings, so what I was unable to discover, I ran the numbers myself.

The ideal length of a web recording: 22 minutes

Stitchery, online radio and webcast webpage, says that the normal audience stays associated for 22 minutes. The study of abilities to focus underpins this number, as well. TED Talks have an 18-minute greatest because researchers accept we can't hold our consideration on a solitary moderator for any more before we look at it.

Greatest day to post a web recording: Tuesday

To discover this end, I pulled the numbers for the Top 25 web recordings in the iTunes store and noticed their distributing plan and the recurrence with which they distributed new digital broadcasts. There was a huge assortment of posting plans among the Top 25, yet a little pattern started to create. A little over half of the web recordings with an ordinary timetable posted from the get-go in the prior week Wednesday. The most well-known single day was Tuesday (which incidentally turns out to be the day when new music hits the iTunes store, probably meaning more visits who may see another digital broadcast).

Best recurrence to post a digital broadcast: Weekly

A little less than half of the Top 25 digital recordings with an ordinary posting plan distribute once every week. The following most regular recurrence is two times seven days. Of the Top 25, just three webcasts didn't have a recognizable timetable for their posting. It appears to be that some distributing beat is liked over no musicality.

Webcasts to gain from; we love taking motivation from others and figuring out how to best handle new media like web recordings. As I referenced up over, a few key destinations are investigating digital recordings, and they're doing as such in truly fascinating manners. Here is a breakdown of five of the best ones and how they do digital recordings.

Tim Ferris – Four Hour Work-Week blog

- Average length of the previous five webcasts: 48 minutes (Ferris sprinkles in short "sound articles" of 10 to 20 minutes close by his more extended digital recordings of longer than 60 minutes)
- Podcast recurrence: Twice every week
- Embedded sound: Lipson
- On iTunes? Indeed
- Full record in the post: No
- Show notes: Yes
- Models:

- The Tim Ferris Show, Episode 12: Dr. Rhonda Patrick on Life Extension, Performance, and Much More
- The Tim Ferris Show, Episode 10: Brian Koppel man, Co-author/Producer of Rounder's, The Illusionist, Ocean's Thirteen

Copy blogger – The Lade webcast

- Average length of the previous five webcasts: 24 minutes
- Podcast recurrence: Weekly
- Embedded sound: Flash player
- On iTunes? Indeed
- Transcript in the post: Yes
- Show notes: Yes

Models:

- Why You Should Curate Content (And How to Do It Right)
- How Freaks and Misfits Can Succeed in Business: A Conversation with Chris Brogan

Failure

- Average length of the previous five webcasts: 44 minutes
- Podcast recurrence: Weekly
- Embedded sound: Lipson
- On iTunes? Indeed
- Transcript in the post: No
- Show notes: Yes

Models:

- Value, Volume, Sales Help or Product Dev.? 5 Tough Listener Questions (FS058)
- 5 Ways to Increase Traffic to Your Site (Plus SEO Insights, FS057)

Persuade and Convert – Social Pros webcast

- Average length of the previous five webcasts: 48 minutes
- Podcast recurrence: Weekly
- Embedded sound: Flash player
- On iTunes? Indeed
- Transcript in the post: No
- Show notes: Yes

Models:

- How Customer Service can Devastate Your Social Media Plans
- How Group on Integrates Social Media and Customer Experience

Online Media Examiner

- Average length of the previous five webcasts: 40 minutes
- Podcast recurrence: Weekly
- Embedded sound: Power Press player
- On iTunes? Indeed
- Transcript in the post: No
- Show notes: Yes

Models:

- Twitter Cards for Blogs: How to Set Them Up
- Marketing Instagram Style: What Marketers Need to Know

Recap

At the highest point of the post, I referenced a couple of the feelings of trepidation that hinder me from contemplating podcasting.

"My voice sounds odd." "I disdain public speaking." Many of the best podcasters started with similar feelings of dread, and once you hear the wide assortment of voices in webcasts, you'll feel alright, as well, about beginning your own. "I don't have the specialized abilities expected to record." Technical abilities are simpler and simpler to drop by these days with the innovation accessible. Also, there's truly hardly any altering to be finished with a straightforward web recording. "The expense of value gear surpasses my little spending plan." Forty dollars ought to be inside most everybody's budget, and that is all you may require to get a practical amplifier set up and start podcasting. Ideally, you're resting easy thinking about those feelings of dread at this point.

What Form does a Podcast Normally Take?

So, you need to begin a digital recording?

Before you start pondering where to have your feed or how to pull in audience members to your show the primary thing you need to do is choose what sort of show you'll be making. You need to pick a configuration. Here's what frequently shocks a few people–a few out of every odd digital recording must be a meeting show. While talking with shows might be perhaps the most mainstream organizes out there presently, there are various approaches to cause a webcast and stick out. Here we'll be covering six primary digital recording organizations to assist you with concluding which will suit your substance best:

- Interviews
- Conversational
- Educational
- Solo-projects
- Non-fiction narrating
- And fiction narrating (at times called digital recording theater)
- The board web recording design

Why picking a podcast design is significant

Building a group of people is about consistency. Consistency in the points you talk about. Consistency in the style of photos on your blog. Consistency in the recurrence of when you'll post a new substance. Furthermore, for digital broadcasts, consistency in your show design.

Associate with your crowd

Offer what you love to interface with your adherents and develop your business with a free Convert Kit account.

Make a free Convert Kit account

Your crowd likes to realize what's in store when they click play on another scene. If your show includes a genuine meeting multi-week, a comedic conversation the following, and a performance bluster the week after, you'll see it harder to acquire footing. Your crowd won't realize how to depict your show when discussing it with others, so it will be hard to get new audience members through close to home suggestions. Furthermore, on the off chance that you start with a thoroughly clean record every week, it will be difficult for you to stay aware of the substance creation as well.

The most famous podcast recording designs

Fortunately, it's genuinely simple to choose an organization once you begin pondering what you need your show to be and the most ideal ways you can carry an incentive to your crowd. How about we dive into the upsides and downsides of the six principle designs.

Interview shows

An exemplary in the podcasting scene, talk with shows for the most part highlight a reliable host (or has) and another visitor every scene. They allow the crowd to be acquainted with a lot of intriguing individuals inside a specialty and gain from their skill. An interview-style show includes a host (or two) who meet another visitor in every scene who brings their exceptional mastery and experience. After a short visitor presentation, the host assumes control over posing inquiries to manage the discussion around the scene's theme attempting to unload their accounts and exercises. Since every visitor is unique, it's ideal to adhere to focal them to keep your show strong.

Pros

Your visitors do the majority of the talking. You simply need to guide the discussion.

Audience members are excusing about little slip-ups (um, likes, and short delays) since they realize you're having a genuine discussion.

Opens your show to another crowd because your visitors advance their appearance on your show, particularly to their fan base.

Your show accesses an assortment of perspectives and assessments, which invigorates conversation and adds an incentive for your audience.

Cons

This is a very famous organization, so you'll battle to stick out.

Talking is an expertise that takes persistence and practice.

Finding another visitor for every scene takes a ton of work.

If you talk with somebody over Skype or Zoom, you're helpless before your association. It might take a couple of attempts to get enough sound for a scene.

You need to do some profound examination of your visitors.

In some sense, you depend on your visitors' capacity to engage and convey data. Your scene will endure if they're troublesome, incoherent, or exhausting, (except if you can redress).

Conversational web recordings

Tuning in to a conversational web recording wants to catch a visit between two companions. Normally these sorts of shows have numerous hosts, and scenes could include conversations on a focused subject (like a collection survey roundtable on Modern Vinyl), or wide scope of things (i.e.-they talk about tech, life, and the Internet on Hello Internet).

These sorts of shows are not difficult to tune in to, simple to record, and will in general be between 30 minutes to an hour-long. Audience members will tune in because they like the hosts' characters and because it is a discussion they're catching, they'll feel more associated with the hosts than to those revealing a story in a verifiable narrating show, for instance.

Pros

- Less construction implies less time spent arranging. You'll simply require a short diagram instead of what you need to talk about in the scene.
- There is consistently somebody to ricochet off of if you run out of comments.

Cons

- To keep your crowd drew in and returning for additional, you'll need to get imaginative and explicit with the themes you talk about.
- Depending on where your co-have is found, you may need to manage to record independently and altering the tracks

together. Furthermore, much the same as with talk with shows, you'll be helpless before Internet associations when you talk over Skype!

Examples:-

The Boa world UX Show:

Boa world is a webcast about the advanced procedure, administration plan, and client experience. It offers commonsense exhortation, news, devices, audit, and meetings with driving figures in the website composition local area. Covering everything from ease of use and plan to advertise and methodology, this show has something for everything.

Err hang Show:

For his most recent undertaking, Al Lesson takes all the things that are coasting in his mind and transforms it into a mixture of pleasure for you. Err hang is only that, everything from narrating to radio dramatization, mainstream society surveys to interviews with the absolute most fascinating individuals on earth. It's a vehicle to grandstand the entirety of Lesson's different gifts.

Instructive shows

Instructive shows frequently have various has, however, are more organized than a conversational digital recording. The scenes will include a particular exercise or takeaway, and audience members will tune in prepared to find out about the current point. Mariah Coz and Megan Mines of The Entrepreneur Show, for instance, produce new scenes consistently showing individuals how to make, run, and sell online courses. Learning by tuning in to a digital recording is extraordinary because you can do it while driving, doing the dishes, strolling the canine they transform a vacation into a profitable time! Furthermore, delivering an instructive show will regularly mean making an evergreen substance that can be burned-through for quite a long time to come.

Pros

- High-esteem data will keep your crowd returning for additional.
- It's not difficult to make supplemental substances like PDF downloads, recordings, or even full courses to get your crowd required on numerous levels.

Cons

- Some subjects can be difficult to instruct without supporting visuals. You can guide audience members to your site for show notes, yet in general, your exercise ought to be not difficult to get a handle on through sound as it were.

Solo-projects

No co-have, no issue! Solo-projects include discourses on a subject that is essential to the maker. The scenes will in general be founded on the maker's insight and could be anything from parody to exhortation based substance. Your crowd will truly feel like they become more acquainted with you, and you can don't hesitate to welcome visitors occasionally for added interest. This digital recording design is genuinely normal. It's utilized by individuals who have a particular sort of aptitude they need to share. There isn't a lot of flourish or arrangement. You just talk into an amplifier. Numerous new podcasters start with this arrangement since it's so basic. All you require to begin is an amplifier and some free altering programming. On the off chance that you pick this digital broadcast design, you'll need to choose the amount you need to design every scene. Some podcasters are agreeable promotion ribbing off a couple of notes, however, others struggle to talk for 30-45 minutes without itemized planning. You may choose to compose a total content for every scene.

Pros

You don't need to depend on anybody's assistance or association. Everything occurs on your timetable and at your speed.

Your crowd comes to know you personally. This is amazing for brand building.

Altering one voice is a lot simpler than altering various tracks.

If you don't care for how you said something, you can say it again and cut out the terrible pieces.

Cons

It's a ton of talking. Representing 30 to 45 minutes is tiring. Also, that is just on the off chance that you record it the first run through. All things considered, you'll talk for an hour or more for every scene.

You don't have anybody to ricochet thoughts off (except if you have an accomplice or group in the background) or help you advance.

In case you're apprehensive behind the mic, you may have to rehearse a piece before recording for your first scene.

Examples of solo podcast format:-

Dan Carlin's Hardcore History:

Dan Carlin takes his irregular perspective and applies it to the past. This isn't scholarly history (and Carlin isn't an antiquarian) yet the webcast's remarkable mix of extreme emotion, mind-blowing portrayal, and Twilight Zone-style turns has engaged great many audience members

The record's the Gist:

The record's The Gist with Mike Pessac. A day by day evening show about news, culture, and whatever else you'll be examining with loved ones around evening time.

Streak Forward:

Streak Forward is a show about conceivable (and not all that conceivable) future situations. Every scene joins the sound show and news-casting to dive deep on expected days to come and uncovers what those prospects may truly resemble. What's to come will be peculiar, so we should prepare for it together.

Podcasts that recount genuine stories

Narrating digital broadcasts are shows that do only that–report on stories from our general surroundings. They could be epic, inside, and out adventures like the genuine wrongdoing examination of Serial. They could investigate the news like The Daily. Or then again maybe they expose more limited size fascinating things like the science-put together narrating concerning Science Vs.

You could disclose to one story across a season (or numerous seasons!) or keep it short and have another story for every scene. In any case, genuine narrating webcasts are an opportunity for you to impart your interests to the world. You'll have to put your agent cap on to make a show in this organization as they typically include brief snippets from various meetings and portrayal to illuminate the crowd regarding what they need to know to get a total comprehension of the story.

Pros

- These kinds of shows are addictive, as demonstrated by the viral accomplishment of Serial. In an article on The Atlantic, Emma Rodeo, an interchanges teacher at the Pompeii Fabre University in Barcelona, said this regarding the matter, "Sound is quite possibly the coziest types of media... you are continually constructing your pictures of the story in your psyche and you're making your creation."

- There's a great deal of opportunity to get inventive with altering and creation.

Cons

- Generally higher creation esteem is normal with this sort of show so there might be an expectation to absorb information when beginning, and you will most likely be unable to deliver shows as routinely.
- These are not the sorts of shows where you can just hit record and talk into the amplifier, there will be all the more arranging and investigating time included.

The board web recording design

A board web recording is like a meeting webcast, however with more individuals. Every scene has a solitary host and a gathering of visitors. For your audience, it seems like catching a natural discussion between companions.

Pros

- Every scene is loaded with one of a kind, fascinating suppositions, and bits of knowledge.
- There's practically no tension on the host because the board of visitors does a dominant part of the talking. A few have just posted a couple of inquiries all through a whole show and let the visitors the greater part of the talking.

Cons

Filling the board with visitors is a huge load of work. You'll need to arrange everybody's timetable. As another podcaster, finding even one visitor is a test.

You'll need to attempt to keep individuals included (so they aren't quiet for 20 minutes), yet you'll additionally need to keep them from talking more than each other.

Your visitors will normally need to discuss a subject for longer than you need them to. You'll need to realize when to slice individuals off and how to proceed onward flawlessly.

There are some specialized difficulties that accompany recording sound from numerous sources.

Examples of the board style digital broadcast design:

Record's Political Gabfest:

Cast a ballot "Most loved Political Podcast" by Apple Podcasts audience members. Stephen Colbert says "Everyone ought to tune in to the Slate Political Gabfest." The Gabfest, highlighting Emily Bazillion, John Dickerson, and David Plots, is the sort of casual and disrespectful conversation Washington writers have twilight over beverages.

The Bean Cast:

The Bean Cast™ is a week after week round table digital broadcast, highlighting notables from the promoting, publicizing, intelligent, and advertising local area. We talk about the most recent industry news with a solid portion of the point of view.

Mother and Dad Are Fighting:

Rebecca Lavoie, Jamila Lemieux, and Dan Kiosk share wins and comes up short and offer exhortation on nurturing kids from the little child to adolescents.

Webcast Theater

In case you're an enthusiast of book recordings or fiction stories when all is said in done, you'll love digital broadcast theater. These are anecdotal stories told across scenes like a TV show, however sound! They include voice entertainers, content, and simply like TV shows they regularly have cliffhangers and interesting plotlines that keep audience members needing to know what's next. In case you're a fiction essayist or into making short movies this could be an extraordinary digital broadcast design for you to investigate and utilize your narrating abilities in another medium.

Pros

- There is a less soaked market for these shows as of now.
- Just like with verifiable narrating shows, these shows can be addictive!
- Cons
- This design is a ton of work. You have all the trouble of composing a story, with the additional work of creating it with voice entertainers!
- As this is a more uncommon show design, it very well may be more enthusiastic to get new audience members to check it out.

Step by step instructions to pick your webcast design. Since you've taken in somewhat more about some unique webcast designs ask yourself.

Which digital broadcast configuration will suit my substance best?

If the appropriate response doesn't promptly come into view, here are some explaining addresses that will help you settle on the choice.

What do you need your crowd to escape tuning in to your show?

On the off chance that the primary concern you need to do is help them learn, at that point maybe an instructive webcast will suit you best. If you will likely engage, at that point maybe a discussion-based show with a clever co-host will function admirably for you. Whatever your objective is, pick a configuration that will be ideal to help accomplish it.

People who listen to a lot of podcasts are different

Which Podcast Enthusiasts and Podcast Newbies

Digital recordings are rapidly turning into a social staple. Somewhere in the range of 2013 and 2018, the percent of Americans over age 12 who had ever tuned in to a digital broadcast bounced from 27% to 44%, as indicated by the Pew Research Center. However, only 17% of Americans have tuned in to a digital broadcast in the previous week. So we needed to know: What recognizes individuals who tune in to digital broadcasts week by week, or even every day, from individuals who just listen sporadically? Do visit and rare webcast audience members have various qualities, necessities, and inclinations? To put it another way, are there various types of webcast audience members?

To investigate this inquiry, Mozilla did a progression of studies and meetings to see how individuals tune in to webcasts — how frequently they tune in, the number of shows they tune in to, what gadgets they use, how they find content, and what highlights of the listening experience matter most to them. This is what we found.

There is a subset of committed, regular webcast audience members... and they listen a great deal

We delivered a short review of digital broadcast listening propensities to an agent of a test of Americans (as selected through Survey Monkey) and a focused on gathering of sound aficionados (disseminated using subedits, for example, r/webcast and r/audio drama and Mozilla's online media accounts). In this overview, we asked individuals how frequently they tune in to digital broadcasts:

How frequently do you tune in to digital broadcasts (across all gadgets)?

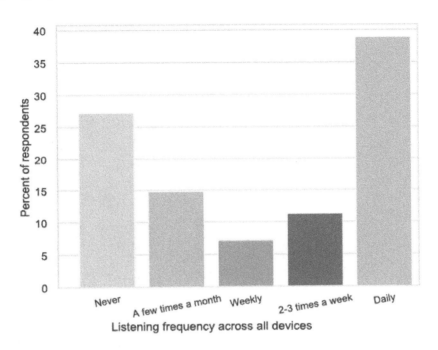

We found that 38% of our survey respondents listen to podcasts daily. Note that we asked this question for each device (i.e., How often do you listen on your phone? On a smart speaker? etc.) The graph above shows the highest listening frequency each person. For example, someone who listens on Alexa a few times a month and on a phone daily would be classified as a daily listener. This could result in an underestimate of each respondent's overall listening frequency.

A bimodal pattern is emerging: People tend to either listen very infrequently (a few times a month) or very frequently (every day). At first, we found it surprising that podcast listenership in our survey was much more common than in Pew's results. However, when we separated the results by the Survey Monkey panel (which is roughly comparable to the general U.S. population) and our Reedit and social media channels, here's what we found:

How often do you listen to podcasts (across all devices)?

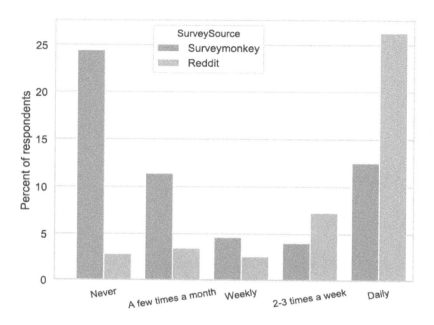

In the Survey Monkey panel, 56% of people at least occasionally listen to podcasts, which is still higher than Pew's findings, but comparable. In contrast, only 91% of the people who accessed the survey via Reedit and Mozilla's social media channels listen to podcasts at least occasionally, and 62% say they listen daily.

The listening distribution of these two populations are inverted. People who follow podcasting-related social media tend to listen a lot. This may seem like an obvious connection, but it suggests that we may find some interesting results if we look at the daily listeners and other podcast listeners separately.

Frequent and infrequent podcast listeners use different technologies

Smartphones are by far the dominant devices for podcast listening. But when we split apart listeners by frequency, we see that smartphone listening is more dominant among daily listeners, whereas laptop and desktop listening is more dominant among monthly listeners: 38% of podcast listeners use smartphones to listen daily; conversely, 27% of podcast listeners use laptops or desktops to listen a few times a month. We also found that frequent podcast listeners are more likely to use multiple types of devices to listen to podcasts.

How often do you listen to podcasts on these different devices?

	Smartphone (iPhone or Android)	Laptop or desktop (Windows, Mac, Linux)	Smart speaker (Amazon Alexa or Google Home)
Daily	38%	8%	3%
Two or three times a week	11%	6%	2%
Weekly	8%	8%	1%
A few times a month	18%	27%	7%

This chart shows how often people listen to podcasts on particular types of devices (smartphones, laptops or desktops, smart speakers) for survey respondents who listen to podcasts at least a few times a month (n = 575).

This distinction in technology use also plays out when we look at the apps/software people use to listen. Apple Podcasts/Apple iTunes is the most popular listening app across all listeners. However, daily listeners use a broader distribution of apps. This could indicate that frequent listeners are experimenting to find the listening experience that best fits their needs. Monthly listeners, on the other hand, are much more likely to listen in a web browser (and may not even have a podcasting app installed on their phone at all). YouTube is popular across all listeners, but proportionately more common with infrequent listeners.

Which podcasting apps do you use?

Frequency of overall listening	Daily	Two to three times a week	Weekly	Monthly
Apple (Podcasts, iTunes)	85	25	22	53
Pocket Casts	44	11	1	2
YouTube	39	15	12	39
Overcast	38	3	0	2
Spotify	34	13	12	12
Google (Play, Podcasts)	32	11	8	17
Podcast Addict	32	8	2	4
Web browser	30	16	11	32
Soundcloud	26	12	0	7
Smart speaker	17	6	3	3
Stitcher	10	1	2	8
Other	76	30	15	19

This chart displays podcast listeners, segmented by listening frequency, and the apps that they use. (Note that we didn't explicitly ask how often people use each app. But we do know that, for example, of the 310 survey respondents who listen to podcasts daily, 85 use Apple Podcasts/Apple iTunes). For all listeners, Apple Podcasts/iTunes is the most popular platform. For weekly and monthly users, YouTube and web browsers are the next most popular platforms.

Why might infrequent listeners be more likely to listen in web browsers and on platforms like YouTube? Perhaps newer and infrequent podcast listeners haven't developed listening routines, or haven't committed to a particular device or app for listening. If they are accessing audio content ad hoc, the web may be easier and more convenient than using an app.

In addition to this broad-scale survey data, we can learn more from in-depth interviews with podcast listeners. Podcasting newbies and podcast enthusiasts have different behaviors — but what about their values? To dig into this question, we interviewed seven people who self-define as podcast enthusiasts, as well as drawing from fieldwork over the summer in Seattle and three European cities to understand listening behaviors. We learned a few key things from those studies, particularly around how people think about subscriptions, and how they learn about new podcasts.

"Memberships" don't completely catch how individuals tune in

While energetic digital recording audience members may buy into a considerable rundown of appears (at 72 among the individuals we talked with), they will in general be committed to a more modest subset of shows, commonly somewhere in the range of 2 and 10 that they tune in to consistently. With these "customary revolution" shows, audience members get new scenes not long after they are delivered and may even return and re-tune into scenes on various occasions. For audience members who have a center arrangement of shows in their ordinary pivot, plunging into a new digital broadcast requires a lot of mental exertion and time. A few people we talked with use memberships as a "save for some other time" highlight, putting away shows that they should hear some out day. However, having a considerable rundown of optimistic webcasts can be overpowering. One audience, for instance, just needs shows "to be before me when I'm in the disposition... So I'm attempting to be careful about buying in and withdrawing. They ought to have an alternate activity that you can do, similar to your rundown of 'when I'm prepared for something new.'"

Associations with digital recordings travel every which way. As one audience portrayed it, consistently, "I will have breakfast. Yet, I unquestionably have experienced stages in my day to day existence. Each day I eat cereal....And then out of nowhere, I disdain that... I sort of feel like my web recording listening goes back and forth and waves that way." One audience we met is, even more, a nibbler, meandering from show to show dependent on themes she is at present inspired by: "I'll simply bounce around, and I'll attempt various things... I normally don't buy-in." For her, the idea of membership doesn't accommodate her listening designs by any stretch of the imagination. These topics demonstrate that maybe the idea of "membership" isn't nuanced enough to catch the mind-boggling and dynamic ways individuals create and break associations with digital broadcast content.

Verbal exchange and webcast cross-advancement are amazing approaches to find content. Web recording aficionados utilize numerous methodologies to sort out what to tune in to, however one methodology overwhelms: When we asked digital broadcast devotees how they find new substance, everyone raised verbally. The interviewees all likewise discovered cross-advancement — when web recording has noticed another show they appreciate — to be powerful because it's a suggestion that comes from a confided invoice. The webcast lovers we talked with depicted extra ways they find content, including perusing top diagrams, hoping to confided in brands, discovering proposals via online media, perusing "most awesome aspect" records, and following a substance maker from another medium (like a creator or a TV star) onto a digital broadcast. Notwithstanding, none of these systems were as normal, or as striking, as a verbal exchange or cross-advancement. Techniques for content revelation can strengthen one another, creating a snowball impact. One audience noted, "I may hear it from like the radio. Kind of a mysterious source first, and afterward I hear it from a companion, 'Similar to gracious I caught wind of that. You just informed me concerning it. I should go look at it now.'" If audience members catch wind of a show from various roads, they are bound to put the time in tuning in to it.

The informal exchange goes the two different ways and digital recording audience members' excitement for discussing webcasts isn't restricted to the different fans. They frequently prescribe digital recordings to non-audience members, both whole shows and explicit scenes that are logically significant. For instance, one interviewee noticed that "At whatever point I have a discussion about something fascinating with somebody I'll say, 'Gracious I heard a Planet Money about that' and I will allude them to it." For continuous web recording audience members, webcast content fills in as a sort of conversational cash.

What does this all mean?

Webcast audience members are not a homogenous gathering. Item planners ought to consider individuals who listen to a little and individuals who listen a great deal; individuals who are new to digital broadcasts and individuals who are submerged in web recording society; individuals who are as yet sorting out some way to tune in and individuals who have assembled solid listening propensities and schedules. These particular gatherings each carry their qualities and inclinations to the listening experience. By considering and tending to them, we can configuration listening items that better fit assorted listening needs. We likewise got some information about listening practices past digital broadcasts. To get familiar with that, look at our partner post, listening: It's not only for the sound.

CHAPTER FIVE

FIND YOUR AUDIENCE OF ONE

Recognizing your intended interest group is one of the fundamental structure squares of an effective promoting system. Now and again everything necessary to turn a business around (and improve ROI) is to investigate who you're promoting to and afterward change your informing and generally speaking technique appropriately. Yet, it's not as simple as you may suspect. Homing in on the correct objective crowd requires some investment, tolerance, and the capacity to investigate your business and your clients. Before you expect you to know your intended interest group, follow these 8 stages. You may very well be astonished by what you reveal

1. Investigate your current clients. Understanding the attributes and buying examples of the individuals who right now purchase your item or administration can uncover a ton about your business.

Investigate the information. Consider profiling and demonstrating your current client rundown to see geographic appropriations, age ranges, way of life factors, and different experiences. Review past triumphs. Recognize missions and informing that have worked before. Who were the possibilities that reacted and how did the mission impact their purchasing conduct?

As of late, Responsorial finished a Marketing Audit for a specialized school that uncovered an astounding crowd knowledge. Perceive how another point of view on the school's showcasing endeavors uncovered a critical undiscovered chance.

2. Burrow further and fragment. Each crowd segment can be additionally divided to be more explicit. For instance, if your item is focused on HR experts, these people can have a wide scope of remarkable qualities. The individuals who work at a huge organization may have some expertise in a specific feature of HR, similar to benefits organization. Other people who work at a more modest organization probably wear numerous caps and may be associated with everything from bookkeeping to acquirement. Make sure to ponder which sections from a crowd of people bunch utilize your item or administration and how.

3. Watch out for the opposition. Watching who your rivals are focusing on and how they are/aren't addressing their requirements can help you further characterize your crowd by focusing on methodology and separate your business. Ask yourself, who is their intended interest group? How are they conversing with them? What are they progressing admirably?

4. Challenge your suspicions. Try not to accept you comprehend your clients. Regardless of whether it's "who you've generally promoted to," it's beneficial to investigate and reevaluate as your business develops. This is the place where leading a careful Marketing Audit can be particularly useful. Look at your essential and optional examination discoveries against your underlying suppositions about your intended interest group. Are there contrasts in socioeconomics? Buy inspiration? Could your crowd be additionally divided to be more exact?

Tune in to your clients. Study as well as meeting your current clients to more readily comprehend their needs and needs. Continuously go with what your clients are saying, regardless of whether it clashes with your unique suppositions.

5. Make crowd personas. Archiving your optimal crowd personas is vital to crystalizing your thoughts and keeping everyone in your association zeroed in on a similar crowd. Viable client personas contain both segment and psychographic data and incorporate insights concerning their way of life, jobs and obligations, correspondence inclinations, and media utilization.

6. Discover your crowd. Since you have a superior comprehension of who your objective possibilities are, you need to sort out where to discover them and how they like to convey. This will assist you with deciding the correct blend of strategies and key messages that will resound with your intended interest group.

Guide out your client venture. By examining how your present clients are finding and drawing in with you now, you'll acquire knowledge into the best touch focuses that end in a deal. Get a head start on planning your client venture.

7. Run test missions and embrace disappointment. You can test everything from points of arrival to standard mail and online media crusades. By testing, you can discover which tactic(s) work best, yet also which features, symbolism, and suggestions to take action to resound most with your intended interest group. Keep in mind, only one out of every odd test will be effective. Truth be told, some of the time the best bits of knowledge come from tests that come up short. Make sure to consistently investigate your outcomes and apply your discoveries to your next mission.

What is a Target Audience?

An intended interest group is a gathering of customers described by conduct and explicit socioeconomics, for example, female extraordinary competitors between the ages of 18 and 25. Target crowds are a mainstay of most organizations impacting dynamic for advertising systems, for example, were to burn through cash on advertisements, how to engage clients, and even what item to work straightaway.

Target crowds are utilized to characterize the purchaser persona of a business, also. Purchaser personas are an agent outline of a business' optimal client, drawn from information that makes up an intended interest group. A portion of these socioeconomics and conduct regions are:

- Location
- Age
- Gender
- Employment
- Income

This data is useful in understanding the client and how they settle on buy choices. Focusing on a particular crowd will likewise help your missions contact the right individuals who will relate most to your organization's message and items.

When discussing an intended interest group, it's a helpful differentiation not to mistake the term for an objective market. While comparative, their distinction is key for advertisers.

Target Market versus Target Audience

Even though both objective crowd and target markets are revolved around dividing clients into gatherings to settle on educated business choices, an objective market is a particular gathering of customers at whom an organization's items are pointed. An intended interest group characterizes that gathering utilizing crowd socioeconomics, interests, and purchasing history. You can portray your objective market by finding your intended interest group. On the off chance that an objective market was "advertisers matured 25-35," the intended interest group would then be something like "advertisers living in Boston, Massachusetts matured 25-35." That was an outline of target crowds. How about we jump into certain points of interest, for example, the various sorts of crowds and how to locate your own.

Sorts of Target Audience

We've momentarily gone over the credits that make up a segment. There is a lot in the showcasing scene — all accommodating in finding the right crowd.

At the point when we talk about kinds of target crowds, we're discussing more approaches to characterize who you're making a mission for. You can section your crowd into gatherings or characterize those further utilizing classes, for example,

- Purchase expectation — Groups of individuals who are searching for a particular item and need to gather more data before doing as such. A few models incorporate shoppers purchasing another PC, vehicle, dress, or TV. This information is vital to perceive how you can all the more likely direct your informing to your crowd.
- Interests — This is information about what individuals are into, similar to interests. Realizing this information causes you to associate with your crowd in a relatable manner and uncover purchaser inspiration and practices. For instance, purchasers who appreciate street trekking as a leisure activity are likely generally keen on new street bicycles in the spring, when the climate is hotter and the street dashing season starts. For instance, on the off chance that you locate that countless potential crowds are keen on voyaging, you can sort out an approach to work that message into your showcasing effort to speak to more expected purchasers.
- Subculture — these are gatherings of individuals who relate to a shared encounter. An illustration of this would be a particular music scene or sort of diversion. Individuals characterize themselves by subcultures, and organizations can utilize those societies to comprehend who they're connecting with. An illustration of arriving at a subculture is considering how they identify with your business, particularly if you have a huge expected crowd. For example, Netflix markets to their

subcultures, individuals who watch explicit sorts of substances, utilizing online media accounts that are coordinated to those subcultures. As you've likely speculated, thinking of an intended interest group includes some exploration, which goes into fleshing out who you need to reach and how you can arrive such that stands apart from contenders.

In case you're prepared to discover yours, follow these means underneath:

How to Find Your Target Audience

1. Use Google Analytics to become familiar with your clients.
2. Create a peruse persona to target blog content.
3. Look at online media examination.
4. Use Facebook Insights.
5. Check on-site execution.
6. Engage with online media crowds.

1. Use Google Analytics to become familiar with your clients.

Google Analytics is a particularly sweeping apparatus and is extraordinary for acquiring segment insights regarding your crowd, just as their inclinations. Review from over that this is basic data that finds an intended interest group. With Google Analytics, you'll have the option to see site bits of knowledge, and it's messed up into various areas, similar to age, sex, and area. These areas are named unmistakably on the dashboard and give beautiful diagrams to you to decipher.

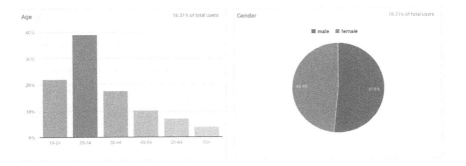

Above is an illustration of the age outline in the Audiences bit of Google Analytics? Notice the breakdown of the numbers and how the charts give you a superb visual. This device can be an incredible resource for getting a truly extraordinary understanding of who's meeting your site and how your substance finds a way into their lives.

2. Make a peruse persona to target blog content.

With peruse personas, you'll always remember who you're composing for. The beneficial thing about peruse personas is that you ought to intently adjust them to your purchaser persona; they ought to be almost indistinguishable.

This is because your blog ought to contain content that will be helpful for peruses. Advertisers presumably need to peruse web journals about advanced media, for instance. It constructs the standing of your organization to buyers. The distinction between a peruse persona and a purchaser persona is that a peruse persona for the most part centers around the difficulties your persona may confront. How might you compose content that tackles those difficulties with blog entries?

For instance, if one of the difficulties you've recognized in your purchaser persona is "Advertising Mario needs to discover an answer for low ROI on advertisement spending," you can utilize a peruse persona to consider content that encompasses helping that challenge.

3. Take a gander at web-based media investigation.

When your adherents are generally drawn in with your online media channels?

Is it when you post an interesting image on Instagram or make a survey on Twitter? By investigating these inquiries, you can get two or three pieces of information into what content your crowd is keen on, hence, filling in one of the parts expected to discover an intended interest group.

Each social channel is extraordinary and has an alternate crowd, so taking a gander at your investigation across all stages is significant. For instance, Twitter will in general have a more youthful crowd, while Facebook will in general have a more established one. On a similar note, Twitter depends on short-structure content, while on Facebook, you can post long-frame substance and recordings.

Instagram is an outwardly based online media stage, so content that is graphically staggering would flourish with the channel. Knowing these things, you can start to design your procedure as needs are.

Investigation can reveal to you who is taking a gander at your profile. Also, they can mention to you what's working and what's not working, content-wise. By posting content your crowd is more inspired by, you can acquire devotees that are in your objective market.

4. Use Facebook Insights.

On the off chance that you have a Facebook page, this apparatus is brilliant for you. Facebook gives each Page an enormous arrangement of experiences, free of charge. These bits of knowledge work correspondingly to Google Analytics — you'll get basic data expected to make an intended interest group. By getting to the People tab on your Insights dashboard, you can see who and from where your guests are. The following is an illustration of how Facebook shows area socioeconomics. It appears to be that an essential area is an east coast, so it's protected to say that piece of the intended interest group for this page is situated in east coast urban areas.

Country	Your Followers	City	Your Followers
United States of America	443	Philadelphia, PA	102
Canada	13	New York, NY	44
Australia	2	Kansas City, MO	14
United Kingdom	2	Denton, TX	13
Austria	1	Richmond, VA	8
Japan	1	Chicago, IL	7
Indonesia	1	Austin, TX	5
France	1	Lancaster, PA	5
		Los Angeles, CA	5
		Toronto, ON, Canada	5

Different zones Facebook centers around incorporate interests and reconciliations with other online media stages, similar to Twitter. The bits of knowledge report reveals to you the way of life of your crowd, for example, on the off chance that they buy things on the web.

Bits of knowledge like these can help you far into your mission arranging, past finding an intended interest group, so it's a beneficial instrument to beware of from time to time.

5. Determine the status of site execution.

Screen your best-and most exceedingly awful performing content zones on your site. Your site can be the prologue to your organization for a ton of your intended interest group, so tidying up what intrigues them is an extraordinary method to pull in more crowded individuals.

By seeing what blog entries or greeting pages are enrapturing your crowd, you can repurpose content that isn't and advance the substance that is. For example, if your blog entry about email advertising was a hit with crowds, share it on your socials to extend your scope.

6. Draw in with online media crowds.

Collaborating with web-based media supporters is so significant because they're your crowd. At the point when you make your purchaser persona, they're the clients you should look to. If you don't have online media accounts yet, make sure to remember this progression.

Ask your devotees what they need to see, use instruments like Instagram Stories and answers to get their reaction for how/what you're doing. Whatever commitment you get, positive or negative, can impact how you pull in more crowded individuals.

For instance, take a stab at tweeting out something that welcomes a CTA, as "Send us an image of your number one outfit to wear with our new caps!" This summons a reaction, reactions you can dissect the language of and impersonate to develop your crowd.

Target Audience Examples

1. Target
2. Light life Foods
3. Apple Music

1. Target

Target separates its substance dependent on social stages. For instance, look at its Twitter account. The language is loose, it draws in clients, and is for the most part outfitted towards a more youthful, millennial group. This is because a large portion of Twitter's client are more youthful.

Alternatively, check out this Facebook post, a partnership with Jessica Alba, an actress who is focused on her family.

This move was probably done because Target's target audience for Facebook campaigns is directed towards families, while the focus is on younger people on Twitter. Target, as a global brand, has different target audiences.

For campaigns, they might focus on a specific audience over another, or for social media channels in general. Target found their target audiences and how they're represented differently and used that to their marketing advantage.

2. Light life Foods

Likewise to the model over, we should see plant-based food organization, Light life Foods. On Instagram, Light life posts great pictures of plans utilizing their items. At times, they work with Instagram influencers in a similar market.

On Light life's Facebook, however, they've invested heavily in video content. This is probably because it's been proven that **video content on Facebook performs extremely well**. Light life is most likely targeting an audience that loves to watch videos on Facebook, whereas on Instagram, they're most likely targeting not only foodies but influencers in their industry.

3. Apple Music

Let's look at how **Apple Music** is reaching their target audience.

On Twitter, the streaming service prides itself on being free of ads, most likely to sway potential audience members away from similar streaming services that don't provide the same benefit. They post playlists and other content that's only reachable by visiting the website.

Most of the Instagram content, however, is videos. It seems as if Apple Music is using their Instagram to post snippets of interviews and other premium content available with a subscription.

Even though the two stages have diverse substance methodologies, the actual substance is in a similar domain, just with an alternate core interest. From this, we can derive that Apple Music likes to adhere to a recipe dependent on where their substance types perform best.

If, for instance, Apple Music found that their meeting sneak peeks perform best on Integra, which is likely why their Instagram is generally video content. This shows that broadening content doesn't need to be a tremendous change like Target and Light life, it can in any case be unpretentious and work.

If you have various objective crowds and just a single advertiser, don't feel as though you need to zero in on each crowd immediately. You can target one crowd for every mission to ensure you truly hit the nail on the head.

Target crowds are intended to draw in customers and give you a smart thought of how to market to them. On the off chance that Vans' method of making various records accommodates your business, pull out all the stops. On the off chance that you have a solitary crowd, you can in any case profit by knowing all that you can about them.

CHAPTER SIX

POSITIONING YOUR PODCAST

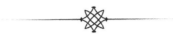

What is a positioning statement?

A situating explanation is a short portrayal of an item or administration and target market, and how the item or administration fills a specific need of the objective market. It's intended to be utilized as an inside instrument to adjust showcasing endeavors to the brand and offer.

Situating explanations are utilized to portray how your item or administration fills a need for your objective market or persona. They're an unquestionable requirement have for any situating system and make a reasonable vision for brand situating.

What is the motivation behind a situating explanation?

The situating articulation goes about as an approach to pass on the offer to the brand's optimal clients while getting down on the brand's character, reason and recognizing highlights.

To make your situating explanation, you'll need to get clear on these parts of your business:

- Who you serve
- What you offer them
- How you offer it
- Why you do what you do
- How this thinks about to what exactly as of now out there

Situating Statement versus Statement of purpose

Your central goal or vision distinguishes the objectives or targets of the brand and can be a significant piece of situating overall. Be that as it may, the situating articulation is something different out and out.

In contrast to a statement of purpose or vision explanation, a situating proclamation is anything but a public-confronting slogan. At its center, it's more extensive than that, summing up the offer, mission, and other situating factors unmistakably and compactly.

Offer versus Situating Statement

The offer and situating proclamation are both key components in a business' advertising technique, notwithstanding, there are contrasts between these two. An incentive is depicted as what separates your item or administration from contenders. It gives a higher perspective outline of the advantages and item or administration gives.

Situating articulations are more extensive, and they're made after you've built up your business' incentive. It likewise distinguishes the essential client advantages and purposes of serious separation.

The Core Elements of Strategic Market Positioning

As referenced before in the article, if you need to create your situating articulation, you should initially have a decent comprehension of your situating all in all. This incorporates characterizing the accompanying center components:

- Target market
- Market classification
- Customer torments
- Brand guarantee
- Brand character and qualities
- Mission

Target Audience

Your intended interest group is the "who" part of your situating. Essentially characterized, it's the gathering of purchasers you're focusing on your item or administrations.

They say that "the wealth is in the specialties," which boils down to the possibility that, regardless of whether anybody can utilize your item or administration, you should in any case be focusing on explicit purchasers so your informing can reverberate. Perhaps the most ideal approach to characterize a strong objective crowd is by considering it regarding a "purchaser persona" or ideal client.

Market Category

A market is involved purchasers and merchants, and a class characterizes a particular section of that market. It where you're contending with different suppliers for the portion of the classification's purchasers.

Regardless of whether your market classification is created and strong or you're essential for a developing business sector or need, you'll need to characterize who the purchasers are in the space, where they're looking for products and ventures, and who right now has their consideration. You'll need to characterize what your opposition offers and how you can situate your image against that opposition.

Client Pains

Client torments are the issues or issues your intended interest group is encountering. Your item or administration will intend to address a client's torment and give an answer.

Brand Promise

Your image guarantee is at last what the intended interest group or purchaser persona stands to acquire from utilizing your item or administration; it's what achievement resembles them if their tormentor issue is settled such that's delightful to them.

Brand Identity

Brand character is the character of your business and incorporates both obvious variables, (for example, logo plan) and less noticeable ones, (for example, qualities or voice). Brand personality is one perspective that will separate you from contenders and help you acquire acknowledgment from your intended interest group.

Qualities

Qualities are the "how you do it" part of your image and serve to make the way of life of your association and affect your intended interest group. They are the elusive techniques with which you execute your central goal and vision.

Mission

Your central goal is the "why you do it" part of your image. Your main goal incorporates your association's objectives, destinations, and approach.

When you have a strong comprehension of personality and situated, you can rotate to making the situating proclamation itself.

Step by step instructions to compose a situating proclamation

1. Keep it brief.
2. Make it novel and essential.
3. Remain consistent with your business' guiding principle.
4. Include a tenable guarantee of what the brand conveys to buyers.
5. Communicate how your business is unique about the opposition.
6. Keep it clean enough for use as a rule to assess whether business choices line up with the brand.

Before you begin composing, ensure you've built up your business' incentive. You'll need to recognize your intended interest group, their problem areas, and how your item can meet their requirements.

What's the guarantee your image gives clients? Also, how might your business convey that guarantee? This is an ideal opportunity to recognize parts of your item or administration that are the essential differentiators from the opposition.

When you have an away from the worth your contribution gives, it's an ideal opportunity to make the situating explanation.

When composing and assessing your situating proclamation, remember the accompanying tips:

1. Keep it brief.

Your image's situating articulation ought to be compact and direct. Focus on close to three to five sentences, if conceivable.

2. Make it special and significant.

This assertion ought to be extraordinary to your organization and the issues you plan to address. While making your situating explanation, make certain to accentuate the unmistakable characteristics of your image.

3. Stay consistent with your business' basic beliefs.

Your image's situating articulation ought to precisely mirror the basic beliefs of your business.

4. Incorporate a dependable guarantee of what the brand conveys to shoppers.

Who does your organization serve? How does your organization serve this gathering? State who your client is and how you help them in your situating articulation.

5. Impart how your business is not the same as the opposition.

A compelling situating proclamation should verbalize what separates a brand from its opposition. Feature your organization's exceptional characteristics and how those characteristics help serve your clients.

6. Keep it clean enough for use as a rule to assess whether business choices line up with the brand.

In practically any situation, your group ought to have the option to adjust key business choices with your image's situating proclamation.

The situating explanation shouldn't be stale — ensure your assertion gives space to develop as your business develops and items change.

Situating Statement Template

For [your target market] who [target market need], [your brand name] gives [main advantage that separates your contribution from competitors] because [reason why target market ought to accept your separation statement.]

The format above can be utilized to help you structure a situating proclamation for your startup or independent venture. Plugin the subtleties of your objective market, organization, and the primary concerns that make your item or administration stand apart from contenders. Every business is special, and it's okay if your assertion doesn't fit the layout precisely, yet make certain to incorporate the central matters.

- A depiction of the objective market.
- A depiction of the objective market needs.
- How your business will address their issues.
- What separates your item or administration from the opposition?
- Why shoppers in your objective market ought to accept your image's cases.

Since situating proclamations are intended to be kept from the public eye, I made model articulations for genuine organizations with conspicuous brands and clear brand situating.

1. Hub Spot

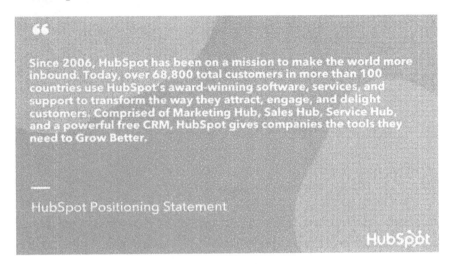

Since 2006, HubSpot has been on a mission to make the world more inbound. Today, over 68,800 total customers in more than 100 countries use HubSpot's award-winning software, services, and support to transform the way they attract, engage, and delight customers. Comprised of Marketing Hub, Sales Hub, Service Hub, and a powerful free CRM, HubSpot gives companies the tools they need to Grow Better.

HubSpot Positioning Statement

HubSpot

Hub Spot's Positioning Statement

Hub Spot Positioning Statement:

Since 2006, hub Spot has been set to make the world more inbound. Today, more than 68,800 all out clients over 100 nations utilize hub Spot's honor winning programming, administrations, and backing to change how they pull in, connect with, and charm clients. Included Marketing Hub, Sales Hub, Service Hub, and an incredible free CRM, hub Spot gives organizations the devices they need to Grow Better.

2. Coca-Cola

Coca-Cola brand situating realistic that incorporates the motto "taste the inclination" with a lady drinking a jug of Coca-Cola

Coca-Cola Positioning Statement:

For people searching for great refreshments, Coca-Cola offers a wide scope of the most reviving choices — each makes a positive encounter for clients when they appreciate a Coca-Cola brand drink. In contrast to other refreshment choices, Coca-Cola items rouse satisfaction and have a constructive outcome in clients' lives, and the brand is seriously centered on the necessities of shoppers and clients.

3. White Dog Distilling

White canine refining's area

White Dog Distilling Positioning Statement:

White Dog Distilling was established in 2016 by the spouse/wife group of Carlo and Alecia Catucci dependent on [passion, soul, and the excursion from grain to glass]. Reinforced via Carlo's experience in material science and Alecia's culinary and item advancement experience, they set out in light of one objective: to create excellent refined spirits that could interest both fledgling soul consumers and long-term devotees the same.

4. The Frozen North Airlines

The Frozen North aircrafts plane

Source: Alaska Airlines

Gold country Airlines Positioning Statement:

We are making an aircraft people love. Every day, we are guided by the basic beliefs of our security, make the best decision, be caring hearted, convey execution, and be momentous grinding away and in our networks. Frozen North Airlines likewise encourages an assorted and comprehensive culture and is an Equal Opportunity Employer.

5. Natural Bath Co.

Natural shower cos. items: cleanser and sanitizer

Source: Organic Bath Co.

Natural Bath Co. Situating Statement:

We realize that what you put on your body is similarly significant as what you put in it — so we've made an honor winning shower and body line utilizing just natural and normal fixings that are protected, powerful and simple to utilize. Our items are an encouragement to back off and enjoy a piece.

6. Amazon

Amazon marking shows a commercial where a man gets an Amazon bundle

Source: Guppy, Amazon

Amazon Positioning Statement:

For customers who need to buy a wide scope of items online with brisk conveyance, Amazon gives a one-stop web-based shopping website. Amazon separates itself from other online retailers with its client fixation, energy for development, and obligation to operational greatness.

7. Effect

Effect's landing page that says: "Hello! We're IMPACT, all that we do is to help you and your association succeed."

Source IMPACT

Effect's Positioning Statement:

At IMPACT, we have upset how inbound promoting is done and instructed organizations by rethinking the office customer relationship through the earth-shattering standards of They Ask, You Answer.

Rather than making a pattern of reliance, wherein our customers are dependent upon us to move the needle and get results, we enable the entirety of the organizations we work with to take responsibility for advanced deals and promoting. Rather than looking for you, we'll "show you how to fish" and devour momentous outcomes for a lifetime. With a wide scope of counseling administrations — content promoting, video deals and showcasing, hub Spot, site system, and plan, and that's only the tip of the iceberg — discover how we can assist you with accomplishing mind-blowing results by turning into the most confided invoice in your space.

8. Beauty counter

Excellence counter brand position realistic that incorporates Beauty counter's perfect guarantee

Source: Beauty counter

Beauty counter Positioning Statement:

Individually, we are driving development to a future where all excellence is perfect magnificence. We are fueled by individuals, and our aggregate mission is to get more secure items under the control of everybody. The figure, advocate, and instruct—that is our witticism for making items that genuinely perform while holding ourselves to unrivaled principles of security. Why? It's this basic: excellence ought to be beneficial for you.

9. Nike

Nike brand realistic that says "you can remove the superhuman from her outfit, however, you can never remove her superpowers" alongside the motto "get it done"

Source: Nike

Nike Positioning Statement:

For competitors needing high-caliber, chic athletic wear, Nike gives clients top-performing active wear and shoes made bar none materials. Its items are the most progressive in the athletic attire industry on account of Nike's obligation to develop an interest in the most recent advancements.

10. Flourish Market

Flourish market items including mayo, truffle, and apple juice vinegar

Source: TechCrunch

Flourish Market Positioning Statement:

Flourish Market is an on the web, enrollment-based market making the most excellent, sound, and practical items accessible for each financial plan, way of life, and geology.

11. Apple

Apple logo

Source: Apple

Apple Positioning Statement:

For people who need the best PC or cell phone, Apple drives the innovation business with the most creative items. Apple underlines mechanical exploration and headway and adopts an inventive strategy to business best practices — it considers the effect our items and cycles have on its clients and the planet.

12. McDonald's

McDonald's announcement that peruses "stuck in a jam? There's a promising end to current circumstances" close to brilliant curves sign

Source: Ad week

McDonald's Positioning Statement:

For people searching for a snappy help café with a remarkable client experience, McDonald's is a pioneer in the cheap food industry, with its benevolent assistance and consistency across a large number of advantageous areas. McDonald's' commitment to improving tasks and consumer loyalty separates it from other drive-thru eateries. Every one of these organizations focuses on an expansive scope of customers and at times it tends to be a smart thought to make separate proclamations for each portion you're focusing on. When your situating explanation (or proclamations) is completely evolved, it's an ideal opportunity to start showcasing your image and building up a predictable message across all stages and all through your business cycle.

Item situating is a type of showcasing that presents the advantages of your item to a specific objective crowd. Through statistical surveying and center gatherings, advertisers can figure out which crowd to target dependent on positive reactions to the item.

Exploration can likewise figure out which item benefits are the most speaking to them. Realizing this data soothes out promoting endeavors and make powerful showcasing messages that drive more leads and deals. It additionally separates the item or administration from the opposition in the commercial center. Item situating is a significant part of any showcasing plan, yet it doesn't need to be restricted to one crowd. For instance, an item may have a fundamental objective crowd and an optional crowd that is additionally intrigued by the item, however maybe in an alternate way. Every crowd will discover the item engaging for various reasons, which is the reason it's essential to tailor advertising messages to zero in on the advantages every crowd esteems most.

Product Positioning

What is Product Positioning?

Item situating can include various components. An item can be situated in a good manner for an intended interest group through publicizing, the channels promoted through, the item bundling, and even how the item is evaluated. For instance, statistical surveying may have uncovered that the item is famous among moms. What do they like about the item? What ought to be featured about the item to draw in them? Also, where should the item be promoted to contact them? With the responses to these inquiries, a successful advertising effort can be made to send advantage driven messages to the intended interest group any place they might be, (for example, Facebook, where focused advertisements can be bought dependent on socioeconomics and interests).

Creation Positioning for Small Businesses

While bigger organizations have the spending plans for broad statistical surveying, independent ventures may struggle thinking of the time or cash to do it top to bottom. Rather than running center gatherings and doing huge loads of examination, an entrepreneur can essentially ask their organization for their feelings. On the off chance that they gather data on clients and their buys, future item situating techniques can be founded on real deals information. This may even be more viable than putting together items situating concerning the assessments of expected clients, for example, in a central gathering, since this situating depends on genuine conduct instead of hypothesis.

All in all, a tremendous promoting spending plan isn't important to exploit statistical surveying and compelling item situating. Understanding the intended interest group and how to convey the advantages of an item to them in a convincing manner is the initial move toward a strong showcasing plan.

Brand positioning

Brand positioning is the way you differentiate yourself from your competitors and how consumers identify and connect with your brand. It's comprised of the key qualities and values that are synonymous with your company. How you differentiate your product or service from that of your competitors and then determine which market niche to fill. Positioning helps establish your product's or service's identity within the eyes of the purchaser.

Marking comprises a bunch of complex marking choices. Significant brand procedure choices include brand situating, brand name choice, brand sponsorship, and brand improvement. Before going into the four marking choices, additionally called brand methodology choices, we ought to explain what a brand is. A brand is an organization's guarantee to convey a particular arrangement of highlights, advantages, administrations, and encounters reliably to purchasers. In any case, a brand ought to rather be perceived as a bunch of discernments a shopper has about the results of a specific firm. Thusly, all marking choices center on the buyer.

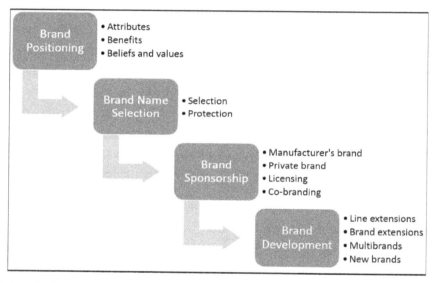

We will investigate every one of these four marking choices.

Marking Decisions - Brand Positioning, Brand Name Selection, Brand Sponsorship and Brand Development Branding Decisions – Brand Positioning, Brand Name Selection, Brand Sponsorship, and Brand Development

Brand Positioning – Branding Decisions

A brand should be situated obviously in objective clients' psyches. Brand situating should be possible at any of three levels:

- On item credits
- On advantages
- On convictions and qualities.

At the least level, advertisers can situate a brand on item credits. Advertising for a vehicle brand may zero in on characteristics, for example, huge motors, extravagant tones, and playful plans. Be that as it may, ascribes are by and large the most un-attractive level for brand situating. The explanation is that contenders can undoubtedly duplicate these credits, removing the uniqueness of the brand. Additionally, clients are not keen on characteristics in that capacity. Or maybe, they are keen on how these credits will help them. That drives us to the following level: Benefits.

A brand can be better-situated on-premise of an alluring advantage. The vehicle brand could go past the specialized item ascribes and advance the subsequent advantages for the client: speedy transportation, way of life thus further.

However, the most grounded brands go past item ascribes and benefits. They are situated on convictions and qualities. Fruitful brands draw in clients on a profound, passionate level. Models incorporate brands, for example, Mini and Aston Martin. These brands depend less on items' substantial credits, yet more on making enthusiasm, shock, and energy encompassing the brand. They have become "cool" brands.

Brand situating establishes the framework for the three other marking choices. Hence, brand situating ought to likewise include setting up a mission for the brand and a dream of what the brand ought to be and do. The brand's guarantee should be straightforward and genuine.

Brand Name Selection – Branding Decisions

When looking at marking choices, the brand name choice might be the most evident one. The name of the brand is possibly your opinion about first while envisioning a brand – it is the base of the brand. Thusly, the brand name choice has a place with the main marking choices. In any case, it is likewise a significant troublesome undertaking. We need to begin with a cautious survey of the item and its advantages, the objective market, and proposed advertising methodologies. Having that at the top of the priority list, we need to discover a brand name coordinating these things. Naming a brand is part science, part craftsmanship, and surely a proportion of impulse. Even though finding the correct name for a brand can be a difficult undertaking, there are a few rules to make it simpler. Alluring characteristics for a brand name include:

- It ought to recommend something about an item's advantages and characteristics. Think about the wadding shine "Never Dull". The brand name shows the advantage of utilizing this item: the treated metal won't ever be dull.
- It ought to be not difficult to articulate, perceive, and recollect. IPod and Nike are positively better than "Shut-in Homunculus" – an attire brand.
- The brand name ought to be unmistakable, so customers don't mistake it for different brands. Rolex and Bugatti are genuine models.
- It ought to likewise be extendable. Consider Amazon.com, which started as an online book retailer however picked a name that would permit venture into different classifications. If Amazon.com had picked an alternate name, for example, books.com, it couldn't have expanded its business that without any problem.
- The brand name ought to interpret of effectively into unknown dialects. The Ford Pinto line had a few battles in Brazil, seeing as it converted into "minuscule male privates". Or then again the Mitsubishi Pajero, which implies in Spanish "man who plays with himself and appreciates it all in all too much". More celebrated: Coca-Cola peruses in Chinese as "female pony loaded down with wax".

- It ought to be equipped for enlistment and lawful security. At the end of the day, it should not encroach on existing brand names.
- Deserving of note is the way that brand name inclinations are evolving persistently. Following a time of picking peculiar names, (for example, Yahoo!, Google) or anecdotal names, the present style is to construct brands around names that convey genuine significance. Names, for example, Blackboard, a school programming, bode well. Nonetheless, with increasingly more brand names and brand name applications, accessible new names can be elusive.

Picking a brand name isn't sufficient. It likewise should be ensured. Numerous organizations endeavor to construct a brand name that will in the end get related to an item classification. Models for these names incorporate Kleenex, Tip-ex, and Jeep. Be that as it may, their prosperity can likewise immediately compromise the organization's privileges to the name. When a brand name turns out to be important for the typical language (called "generalization"), it isn't secured any longer. Hence numerous initially ensured brand names, for example, ibuprofen, Walkman (by Sony), and numerous different names are not secured any longer.

Brand Sponsorship – Branding Decisions

Marking choices go past settling on brand situating and brand name. The third of our four marking choices is brand sponsorship. A producer has four brand sponsorship choices.

Marking Decisions - Brand Sponsorship Options Branding Decisions – Brand Sponsorship Options

An item might be dispatched as a maker's image. This is additionally called public brand. Models incorporate Kellogg selling its yield under the own image name (Kellogg's Frostiest, for example) or (Sony Bra via HDTV). The maker could likewise offer to affiliates who give the item a private brand. This is likewise called a store brand, a wholesaler brand, or an own-mark. Ongoing harder monetary occasions have made a genuine store-brand blast. As buyers become more cost cognizant, they additionally become less brand-cognizant and will pick private brands rather than set up and frequently more costly producer's brands.

Additionally, makers can pick authorized brands. Rather than burning through millions to make their image names, a few organizations permit names or images recently made by different makers. This can likewise include names of notable famous people or characters from mainstream films and books. For an expense, they can give a moment and demonstrated the brand name. For instance, merchants of youngsters' items frequently append character names to attire, toys, etc. These authorized character names incorporate Disney, Star Wars, Hello Kitty, and some more. At long last, two organizations can unite and co-brand an item. Co-marking is the act of utilizing the set up brand names of two distinct organizations on a similar item. This can offer numerous favorable circumstances, for example, the way that the joined brands make more extensive shopper bid and bigger brand value. For example, Nestlé utilizes co-marking for its Espresso espresso machines, which convey the brand names of notable kitchen hardware producers, for example, Krupp's, DeLong HI, and Siemens.

Brand Development – Branding Decisions

Marking choices at long last incorporate brand improvement. For creating brands, an organization has four options: line augmentations, brand expansions, multi-brands, or new brands.

Marking Decisions – Brand Development Options

Line augmentation alludes to stretching out a current brand name to new structures, sizes, shadings, fixings, or kinds of a current item class. This is a minimal effort, generally a safe approach to present new items. In any case, there are the dangers that the brand name gets overextended and loses its particular importance. This may befuddle customers. A model for line expansion is when Coca-Cola presents another flavor, for example, diet cola with vanilla, under the current brand name.

Brand augmentation additionally expects a current brand name, yet consolidates it with another item classification. Accordingly, a current brand name is stretched out to another item class. This gives the new item moment acknowledgment and quicker acknowledgment and can save significant publicizing costs for building up another brand. Nonetheless, the danger that the expansion may befuddle the picture of the principal brand ought to be remembered. Likewise, if the augmentation comes up short, it might hurt customer perspectives toward different items conveying a similar brand name. Therefore, a brand augmentation, for example, Heinz pet food can't endure. Yet, other brand expansions function admirably. For example, Kellogg's has expanded its Special K solid breakfast oat bran into a total line of grains in addition to a line of bread rolls, bites, and sustenance bars.

Multiband implies advertising various brands in a given item class. P&G (Procter and Gamble) and Unilever are the best models for this. In the USA, P&G sells six brands of clothing cleanser, five brands of cleanser, and four brands of dishwashing cleanser. Why? Multi branding offers an approach to building up unmistakable highlights that appeal to various client fragments. In this manner, the organization can catch a bigger piece of the pie. Be that as it may, each brand may acquire just an exceptionally little piece of the overall industry and none might be entirely beneficial.

New brands are required when the force of existing brand names is disappearing. Additionally, another brand name is proper when the organization enters another item class for which none of its present image names are suitable.

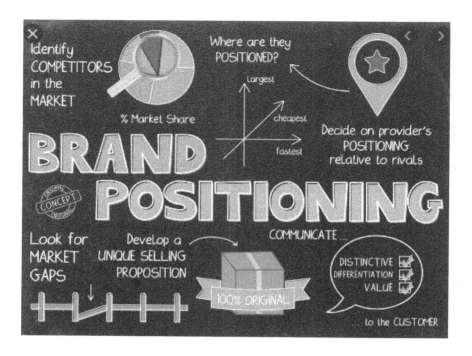

Not very far in the past, "digital recordings" were fascinating. Presently, they're all over. Their capacity to intensify a brand, advance data and engage practically any crowd is underscored by their sheer expansion. 900,000 last time anyone checked. Furthermore, checking.

Simple to make, simple to hear. That is the uplifting news - and the awful. Since nobody can get 1,000,000 webcasts while in transit to work. So how might they discover - and for what reason will they tune in - to yours? Here are 5 Steps to Success from our Loma studio group to help answer that question. We've created digital broadcasts that have accomplished #1 class rankings.

1. Examination. Examination. Exploration. (Furthermore, when you figure you've done what's necessary, do somewhat more.)

This is the place where you would prefer not to be innovative - you should be realistic. Fundamental exploration is vital, particularly for amateurs. It directs the diagram for the whole podcasting measure. Tune in to parcels (and heaps) of digital broadcasts that are in the space you need to involve. Prominent models are a decent spot to begin, yet digital broadcasts with more modest impressions can be similarly as accommodating (regardless of whether just to exhibit what not to do). Tune in for contrasts in sound quality, length, tone, the quantity of members, the number of scenes have been delivered and at what recurrence. Focus on everything!

2. Situating – Here are simply the correct inquiries to pose

Regardless of whether assembling another brand or graphing a new way for your current voice, effectively situating your message to the commercial center will pay quick (and long haul) profits. This is the place where procedure and vision meet - before any chronicles are made. So before you begin looking for new earphones, (consider the Sony MDR-7506 btw, yet trade out the ear cushions. Furthermore, no, we're not a paid endorser) you need to consider your crowd.

Who might you want to hear your digital broadcast and What would they Like to hear? Answer this multi-part question, and afterward answer it 5 additional occasions. Presently, pause and consider new ideas; answer it 5 additional occasions. OK, presently we can proceed onward. Next ask yourself what issue would you say you are settling? What makes you remarkable/your differentiator? Is your web recording for diversion/enlightening/instructive? The responses to these inquiries will give you a smart thought of the situation of your home in Podcast Ville.

The adaptable length of digital recordings takes into consideration both subject explicit and close point conversations that give extraordinary occasions to help brands and associations build up and expand their voice. Scenes can go from 2-hour talks with down to 15-minute "in the field" stories, the decision is yours. Furthermore, the conversational idea of a digital recording takes into account the consideration of integral supporting substance in a more natural style. Presently an ideal opportunity to decide key zones and level of center, since this progression will graph the 'guide' for your digital recording (and arrangement) achievement.

3. Casing your message

You know your central goal, and your crowd. Presently, how regularly would it be a good idea for you to contact them?

Webcasts can be delivered quarterly, month to month, week after week, day by day... or even 30 scenes immediately (not prompted). There are essentially no guidelines which is fun be that as it may, it very well may be somewhat overwhelming. So how about we get this thing on rails. Characterize an overall delivery plan. It will help characterize different factors of the digital broadcast (length, financial plan, hosts and visitors.) Consistently overview the serious scene inside your picked space (sorry - more exploration) and casing the distinctive informing out there against what you desire to accomplish. This is the place where makers like Loma practice, exploring the current media environment for ideal outcomes. Connect on the off chance that you need some help* here. (*not suggested for those intrigued by 'unremarkable' or 'normal,' a few limitations apply, see site for subtleties. Furthermore, presently, back to our standard planned program.)

4. Specialty your voice (and climate)

Presently the inventive vision gets genuine. Tone is critical and should mirror the sensibilities of your intended interest group. Is it fun? Is it genuine or sensational? At a basic level, a web recording weds early "radio days" with the account dynamic of a cutting edge film. It's tied in with narrating, and there are numerous approaches to tell yours.

Digital recordings, as regular discussions, have a wide assortment of host/visitor conversation elements. Two individuals may draw in for 60 minutes, a meandering conversation wherein the guest(s) IS the theme. Far off chronicle is another choice that can oblige different hosts as well as visitors. Convincing areas make an additional feeling of commitment, while a studio climate is likely better for control and cost. Whichever course you make in Stride 4, ensure the innovative is lined up with the diagram you've set up in Steps 1-3. Which carries us to…

5. Brand is everything!

The "it" factor. It's difficult to characterize, however we as a whole know it's there (or not). This is marking. How about we ensure you get "it" right. Creating a digital broadcast that draws in audience members takes in excess of an amplifier and 'radio' voice. Regularly neglected is the visual marking, 'logline' and going with showcasing materials needed for a delivery across significant stages. Get likely audience members to "lean in" by briefly (and aesthetically) depicting the item you're making and worth they'll get. In spite of the fact that it's a sound arrangement, visuals can assume a significant part in passing on the 'vibe' of your digital broadcast. It is anything but a poorly conceived notion to make the 'look' even before you characterize the creation. (On the off chance that it works in Hollywood, it can work for you.)

Furthermore, solid plan has a necessary impact in making a fruitful web recording. From exceptionally easy to deliberately arranged sound, the sonic space of podcasting permits a great deal of space for inventiveness yet set a steady pace or style. This will help bookmark and characterize the digital broadcast in the audience's memory. In any case, decide in favor of straightforward and reliable instead of expound and continually evolving.

Last, yet absolutely not least, how about we all recall that a quality webcast is a mix of craftsmanship and science. As a generally new medium, advancement and innovativeness stay central, yet your chances of accomplishment will be improved by following the essential "obstructing and handling" tips recorded here. Presently…. the warm up is finished….it's an ideal opportunity to get in the game!

What is your show's Unique Show Positioning?

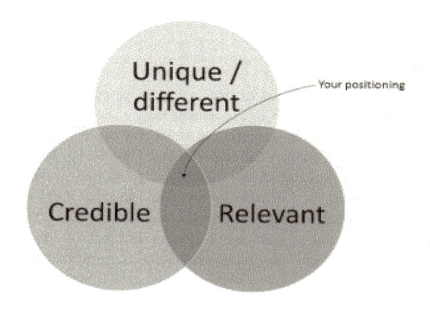

Your positioning

Planning Your Competitive Position

By Richard A. D'Aveni

From the Magazine (November 2007)

Rundown. Reproduce: R0711G a value advantage situating map causes you to see, through your clients' eyes, how you're item contrasts and every one of its rivals in a market. You can draw such a guide rapidly and impartially, without falling back on expensive, tedious customer overviews or subjective...more

Two months. That is all that isolated the dispatch of Apple's progressive iPhone, on June 29, 2007, and Motorola's cutting edge Razr2 (articulated Raze Squared) cell phone, on August 24. Before divulging the replacement to the raze, which PC World magazine in 2005 positioned twelfth on the elite of the 50 biggest devices of the previous 50 years, Motorola's top supervisory crew was more stressed than expected. With deals of the American correspondence monsters other cell phones tightening, the organization's destiny laid soundly on the Razr2. Also, senior heads like administrator and CEO Edward J. Zander contemplated whether the iPhone had changed the serious elements of the market in manners they hadn't anticipated. Had the iPhone made another specialty or would it take the Razr2 head-on? What amount extra could they charge for the Razr2's new highlights? Should Motorola hype the Razr2's commotion sift innovation, which it had protected? The heads couldn't sit tight for the consequences of center gathering meetings or test reviews. They required a quick, yet dependable method of catching changes that were arising on the lookout so they could finish the technique rapidly. Like Motorola, most organizations need to construct new upper hands and obliterate others' preferences quicker than they used to. As advancement plagues the worth chain, they should move rapidly starting with one serious position then onto the next, making new ones, deteriorating old ones, and coordinating opponents'. The cycle is tumultuous and shaky. Senior chiefs urgently need new apparatuses to assist them with breaking down their own and other players' serious situations in hypercompetitive business sectors. One approach to do that is to follow the connection among costs and an item's critical advantage after some time. In any case, it is difficult to deal with either advantages or costs. Most clients can't recognize the highlights that decide the costs they are eager to pay for items or administrations, as per a 2004 review by Stativity, a worldwide exploration, and counseling firm. More terrible, half of the salesmen don't have the foggiest idea what ascribes legitimize the costs of the items and administrations they sell.

On the off chance that clients don't have the foggiest idea what they're paying for, and supervisors don't have a clue what they're charging for, it's practically outlandish for organizations to distinguish their serious positions. At whatever point I've requested senior heads to plan the situations from their organization's brands and those of key adversaries, we end up confounded and disheartened. Various heads place their association's contributions in various spots on a value advantage map; hardly any know the essential advantage their item offers, and they all overestimate the advantages of their contributions while belittling those of adversaries. The absence of comprehension about serious positions is obvious in businesses, for example, purchaser gadgets, where the quantity of highlights makes examinations convoluted; in business sectors like PC equipment, where advancements and techniques change constantly; and when items, for example, protection arrangements, are theoretical.

At whatever point I've requested senior chiefs to plan the situations from their organization's brands and those of key opponents, we end up confounded and terrified.

Seven years back, I thought of a way organizations could catch serious positions graphically to fill in as the reason for system conversations. Drawn by utilizing straightforward measurable investigation, a value advantage situating map gives bits of knowledge into the connection among costs and advantages, and tracks how serious positions change over the long haul. Heads can utilize the apparatus to benchmark themselves against rivals, analyze contenders' systems, and estimate a market's future, as we will find in the accompanying pages. By making a precise guide of the serious scene, organizations can likewise get everybody in the association on the same wavelength. During my counseling and exploration work, I have applied this apparatus over 30 enterprises, including cars, progressed materials, fake sugars, cell phones, cafés, retailing, turbines, tires, bikes, and ships. Allow me to tell you the best way to make and peruse a situating map.

Drawing Positioning Maps

In its easiest structure, a value advantage situating map shows the connection between the essential advantages that an item gives to clients and the costs of the relative multitude of items in a given market. Making such a guide includes three stages.

Characterize the market.

To draw a significant guide, you should determine the limits of the market where you're intrigued. To begin with, recognize the customer needs you to wish to comprehend. You should project a wide net for items and administrations that fulfill those requirements, so you're not walloped by new participants, innovations, or bizarre contributions that deal with those necessities. Second, pick the country or locale you wish to examine. It's ideal to restrict the geographic extent of the examination if clients, contenders, or how items are utilized vary generally across borders. At long last, choose if you need to follow the whole market for an item or just a particular portion, on the off chance that you wish to investigate the retail or discount market, and in case you will follow items or brands. You can make various guides by changing these casings of examination.

Pick the cost and decide the essential advantage.

Whenever you've characterized the market, you need to indicate the extent of your examination of costs. You have verifiably concluded whether to concentrate retail or discount costs when you picked which market to zero in on, however, you should likewise think about other estimating boundaries. You should pick whether to look at beginning costs or costs that incorporate life cycle costs, costs with exchange costs or without them, and the costs of unbundled or packaged offers. These decisions rely upon the measuring stick that clients use in settling on buying choices in the market under investigation. Make sure to be steady about the value definition you use while gathering information.

Recognizing the essential advantage—the advantage that clarifies the biggest measure of the difference in costs—can be muddled. An item offers a few advantages: fundamental capacities, extra highlights, solidness, usefulness, style, convenience, etc. Additionally, organizations normally separate items by zeroing in on an unexpected advantage in comparison to contenders do. Nonetheless, the achievement of procedures relies upon the worth that clients, not organizations, place on highlights. To confirm that esteem, you should initially draw up a top-notch of the advantages offered by all the various items or brands on the lookout and assemble information on how clients see those advantages.

You should utilize fair information, instead of depending on gut intuition or top supervisors' feelings, so you gauge the advantages' worth accurately. There are more wellsprings of hard information today than any time in recent memory. You can draw on the item appraisals of autonomous associations, for example, Consumers Union, J.D. Force, and Edmunds, just as on government organizations, similar to the U.S. Ecological Protection Agency and the U.S. Public Highway Traffic Safety Administration. Shopper guides, for example, Zagat and Michelin; sites, for example, Trip Advisor and the Tire Rack; and exchange distributions, similar to Ward's Auto World, additionally give data on items and administrations. Mechanical indexes distribute point by point item particulars, particularly for innovative and modern products. Wholesalers frequently gather insights concerning item benefits. For instance, vehicle sellers assemble guarantee data to follow how dependable cars are. Your R&D division likely tracks logical information: Consumer hardware producers, for example, gather data on sound and video frameworks' generation quality.

Whenever you've accumulated information on items' advantages and costs, utilize a relapse examination to discover which advantage clarifies the vast majority of the fluctuation in items' costs. Utilizing relapse investigation is more solid than asking individuals the amount they are happy to pay for each element since shoppers frequently can't clarify how they settle on their decisions and they regularly don't do what they say.

Relapse investigation analyzes the connection between a needy variable (for this situation, cost) and a few free factors (item benefits) and makes a numerical model of that relationship called the relapse condition (for this situation, the value advantage condition). Numerous product bundles—Excel, SAS Analytics, and SPSS 15.0

for Windows, for example—permit heads to perform relapse examinations. At the point when the product finds the relapse condition, it will likewise yield a gradual r-square measurement for every autonomous variable. That measurement shows the degree to which each profit adds to the distinctions in the costs of contending contributions while controlling for the effect of any remaining advantages. The advantage with the most noteworthy steady r-settle outstanding balances for a greater amount of the variation in costs than different advantages, so it's the main driver of cost. On the off chance that few advantages relate with each other, that proposes they together impact value contrasts. In such cases, you can join them into a solitary advantage by making a list or a scale—a typical practice in promoting research.

Plot positions and draw the normal value line.

At the point when you have distinguished the essential advantage, you are prepared to draw a situating map by plotting the situation of each organization's item (or brand) in the commercial center as indicated by its cost and its degree of essential advantage. Such situating guides might be a misrepresentation, however, they show the overall places of contenders on a typical scale.

At long last, you should draw the normal value line—that is, the line that best fits the focuses on the guide. The line shows how much clients hope to pay on normal to get various levels of the essential advantage. What's more, the line's incline discloses to us the amount more a client is probably going to pay for a more elevated level of the essential advantage. You can discover the line that best fits the information by taking the incline related to the segment of the value advantage condition that connects the essential advantage to costs. Or then again you can take a gander at the guide and draw a line that runs generally through the center of the haze of focuses; as such, a large portion of the focuses should lie over the line and half should lie beneath. Examination shows that in practically all ventures, a straight line that ascents to the correct fit the information best. Bended lines and adversely slanted lines are conceivable outcomes in principle, yet they portray fleeting wonders. Markets will in general unite on a similar cost for each advantage, and individuals will in general compensation more for a more elevated level of advantage, so those patterns make a straight line with a positive slant. Items lie on one or the other side of the line not coincidentally but rather given organizations' methodologies. Ventures position an item or brand over the line to augment benefits, which they can do by just bringing the cost up in the short run. They can likewise do as such by alluring clients to address a greater expense for attractive optional advantages. Organizations can space their contributions beneath the line to boost a piece of the pie by just charging not exactly expected, or they may drop some optional advantages to pull in value touchy clients. At times, an item's auxiliary ascribes may diminish its cost beneath what individuals would, as a rule, pay for that degree of advantage. For instance, if a without calorie sugar leaves a lingering flavor, individuals will pay less for a similar degree of eating fewer carbs advantage the sugar gives them. Accordingly, deviations in cost above or beneath the line are brought about by the additional or discounted esteem related to optional advantages or estimating methodologies intended to milk or construct a piece of the pie.

Allow me to show the interaction and reasons for drawing a situating map by returning briefly to the difficulties that Motorola looked in dispatching the Razr2. Toward the beginning of June 2007, my examination partner and I went through seven days gathering information from public sources on 40 "opened" cell phones, which work with the calling plans of numerous U.S. cell specialist organizations. We additionally accumulated all the information we could discover on the iPhone. We drew up a top-notch of the telephones' highlights, shopper appraisals of those highlights, and retail costs. A relapse investigation demonstrated that cutting-edge usefulness represented a large portion of the distinction in the costs of cell phones. By cutting edge usefulness, I mean innovative highlights like the capacity to play music in the MP3 design and to snap high-goal photos, the presence of complex email programming, and a QWERTY console. Progressed usefulness represented 68% of the variation in costs, and as indicated by my investigation clients paid on normal $28 more for each high-level element in a cell phone.

Two different advantages added to value contrasts, but less significantly: show quality (shading, high-goal screens, and contact screens) and progressed availability (Bluetooth, 3G, and Wi-Fi innovations). These three advantages together represented 80.5% of the distinction in the costs of handsets. In opposition to the famous insight that battery life and the clearness of sound while settling on and accepting decisions matter to buyers, I found that opposition had diminished those to cleanliness factors (demonstrated by the way that their r-square qualities were incredibly low). Even though Motorola has protected an innovation that channels out foundation commotion from discussions, the outcomes proposed the organization should reconsider before underlining that as one of the Razr2's principal benefits.

At the point when I planned the serious places that different items involved in the commercial center and drew the normal value line, I discovered five bunches of cell phones (see the display "Planning the Cell Phone Market"). Motorola had admirably spread its wagers, situating items in four of the five gatherings. Like the wide range of various cell phone makers, it had no item in the ultra-premium fragment that the iPhone is by all accounts spearheading, yet it had situated items on the two sides of the normal value line. For instance, in the midrange gathering, the Razo V3c was actually on the line, though the Razo SLVR L7 and Razo V360 were underneath it. Sony Ericsson, Samsung, and LG had likewise situated gadgets underneath the line, which proposed that the section was getting packed and costs would before long go into free-fall. The LG VX9800 had situated itself over the line, due to the additional estimating force of its wonderful shading show.

Plotting costs against the essential advantage items offer in a market makes it simple to perceive how that market looks to clients. This value advantage situating map recommends there were five fragments in the U.S. cell phone market when Apple dispatched the iPhone in June 2007, cutting out another ultra-premium specialty. That was fleeting, however, as Apple immediately dropped the cost by $200 in September. The move, which may have been foreseen considering Apple's iPod system, obviously squeezes numerous major parts in the super premium portion.

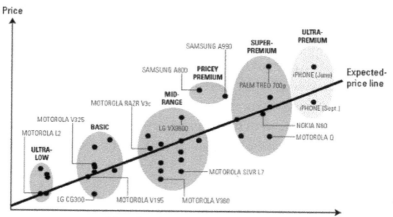

Planning the Cell Phone Market

Plotting costs against the essential advantage items offer in a market makes it simple to perceive how that market looks to...

The iPhone will significantly affect the super-premium fragment; Motorola's Q, for instance, will be outmatched. While a few clients are probably going to defer the acquisition of cell phones until they can bear the cost of the iPhone, it is probably not going to affect the remainder of the market—at first. Notwithstanding, Motorola will confront a hardened test since Apple is conveying its iPod technique in the cell phone market.

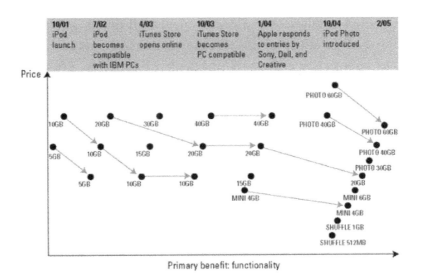

On the lookout for downloadable-music players, Apple began in an exorbitant cost, high-benefits position yet quickly dropped down and to one side by bringing down the cost for a similar essential advantage (see the show "How Apple Set the Pace with the iPod"). In like vein, the organization cut the cost of the iPhone by 33% toward the beginning of September, two months after its dispatch. If Apple keeps on utilizing a similar system, the iPhone will move rapidly from the ultra-premium to a midrange position. The Razr2 will at that point become an essential telephone since it doesn't offer the iPhone's high-level capacities.

How Apple Set the Pace with the iPod

Plotting costs against the essential advantage over the long run for a product offering can make shifts in the market system understood. In this model,

Macintosh likewise made a full line of iPod items, making it extreme for opponents to discover uncontested spaces. On the off chance that it does likewise with the iPhone, Motorola will before long need to battle with a line of iPhones that will coordinate Motorola's full line of Razors. Motorola would progress nicely, all things considered, to push those of the Razr2's high-level capacities that purchasers esteem most, as opposed to adding more optional highlights. For example, having a haptic touch screen on the Razr2 is a novel advantage. Do clients need it? Maybe—however it comes next to the high-level usefulness they are additionally ready to pay for.

Deciphering Positioning Maps

Situating maps assist organizations with entering the haze that covers the serious scene. They can pinpoint the advantages that clients esteem, find vacant or less serious spaces, distinguish openings made by changes in the connection between the essential advantage and costs, and permit organizations to envision opponents' systems. At the point when deciphered inside the setting of industry and client information, they help clarify why a few undertakings' items and brands perform in a way that is better than others do.

Esteeming theoretical advantages.

Numerous organizations, particularly in mechanical business sectors, try to hold clients by offering elusive advantages. Keeping that in mind, they go through a lot of cash to offer strengthening administrations without knowing whether clients need them enough to pay for them. This regularly ends up being a channel on corporate assets. Organizations can dodge the issue by figuring the expenses they procure for immaterial auxiliary advantages.

That was driven home to me when my associates and I led an examination of the U.S. cruiser market. As indicated by a relapse examination, in the mid-2000s, varieties in motor force, as estimated by dislodging, clarified a significant part of the distinction in bike costs. However, a situating map indicated that, in 2002, the vast majority of Harley-Davidson's models procured huge charges contrasted and rival items. By and large, for Harleys than they accomplished motorbikes from Honda, Yamaha, Kawasaki, and Suzuki, even though the Japanese Big Four offered 8% to 12% more motor force. Since we the affected costs of every actual element and characteristics, we inferred that the premium was most likely the consequence of the immaterial optional advantages the organization offered, for example, the picture made by enrollment in the Harley Owners Group (HOG) and clothing from Harley-Davidson's Motor Clothes. These advantages had helped Harley-Davidson make the feeling that its clients were rebels, that they delighted in a daring way of life, and that they had a place with a macho club. Harleys had accomplished faction status, particularly among the gen X-err age.

Notwithstanding, the 2004 situating map uncovered an alternate picture. The cost of a Harley was as yet higher than that of identical Japanese motorbikes, however, it not, at this point instructed the most elevated expenses on the lookout. New American adversaries, for example, Victory and Big Dog, procured a 41% premium over Harley-Davidson for a similar degree of motor limit. The market chief was leaving cash on the table, perhaps because its picture not, at this point spoke to clients. We estimated that both Generation X and Generation Y shoppers were considering to be as their dad's motorbike and that numerous ladies detested its terrible kid picture. Victors'.

CHAPTER SEVEN

CHOOSING A PODCAST FORMAT

When podcasting first went ahead of the scene, there was a whirlwind of theory concerning the eventual fate of radio and if podcasting would stay as a feasible strategy for burning-through sound substance.

Pundits were torn. Some said that podcasting would mean the demise of radio, while others believed that podcasting would drop of the substance of the Earth. Sometimes before a meeting, somebody got some information about this subject. My solution to their inquiry was that podcasting would not vanish and radio would need to adjust to contend with the new medium and its phenomenally different substance and time-moving comfort for audience members.

From my vantage point, podcasting has developed, has acquired acknowledgment, and keeps walking toward the basic reception of the greater part as a medium that can be depended upon for openness, assortment, and above all, on interest webcast utilization. Brain you, Radio is getting up to speed by podcasting a portion of their projects for nothing and a grouping of TV shows can be bought in the iTunes store for a dollar apiece.

Possibly one day, the new discussion will be "Podcasting or Broadcasting?" Currently, we're working out as a people whether we would prefer to drink "Coke or Pepsi" and utilize a "Macintosh or PC", yet this discussion will begin stewing and maybe as of now has in certain working environments and water openings. I realize that large numbers of the web recordings that I right now buy in to just have an online presence, and that being said, I wouldn't have any desire to surrender them, particularly since they are so compact... Pop your MP3 player into your PC, update the playlist, and off you go, most loved projects that are agreeable and accessible on interest.

Tuning in to various sorts of webcasts can be an approach to take part in a type of narrating that permits you to simply pause for a moment and tune in. It very well may be a pleasant break from gazing at a screen or the pages of a book, and can likewise be a path for the web recording host to assume you to another position – if just for an hour or two.

Webcasts are on the ascent with the quantity of digital broadcast audience members expanding 23% in a year. Put another way, from 2016 to 2017, the quantity of digital recording audience members hopped from 13 million to 16 million, and those numbers are simply set to develop throughout the next few years.

So what causes to digital recording resound with its audience members and keep them tuning in after quite a while after week? It's a mix of the arrangement of the digital recording, and the vocal characteristics of the webcast have. Investigating the credits of the absolute most famous webcasts and their hosts can assist you with finding how you can transform your web recording into a broadly tuned show. Here is a portion of the various sorts of digital recordings you can imitate, the most top of the line webcasts accessible on iTunes and the vocal characteristics and styles of the webcast has that make them so captivating and make them great questioners.

4 Different Types of Podcasts

1. Verifiable Narrative Storytelling

This is presumably perhaps the most well-known web recording designs, however, it's precarious to dominate. This space will in general be overwhelmed by columnists who are extraordinary at getting top to bottom and clever data from their subjects. These digital recordings retell the genuine accounts of others using brief snippets from the interviewee, just as a layer all alone editorializing of the current tales.

Here are perhaps the most mainstream instances of a verifiable account webcast:

This American Life

Podcast host: Ira Glass

This American Life is 60 minutes in length week by week radio-program transformed into a web recording. The webcast covers generally genuine and at times anecdotal stories that meet up under another subject every week. The show is heard by over 2.2 million audience members week after week. For what reason is a digital recording so mainstream?

Portrayal Style

The pod recording host is Ira Glass, an essayist, maker, correspondent, and supervisor (among numerous different characteristics). His narrating is one of an all-knowing storyteller – he seems to know things about the characters in the story that they might not have completely dealt with yet. He permits the brief snippets of the characters to represent themselves, yet sums up the activities of the characters such that brings the crowds somewhere inside the character's inspirations – and snares them all the while.

Example: In an account of a man attempting to move to America from Somalia, Ira says, "Truly, more than anyone he knew, Abdi had been fixated on America since he was a small child."

Vocal Qualities of the Podcast Host

Even though Ira has been a radio personality for a long time, his voice isn't the ordinary, radio-commentator voice you might be hoping to hear. He has portrayed his voice as a piece "geeky" and "nasally," all characteristics that cause him to appear to be more agreeable. As it were, you sense that you are hearing a story from somebody you know and not somebody who may appear to be somewhat unattainable (like a roaring radio voice would be). The way that Ira seems like the man-nearby aides attract audience members.

Other mainstream instances of verifiable story webcasts:

- Work in Progress
- Startup
- Radio lab

2. Half and half

A half and half digital recording will in general be one that has a set host, however, regularly has different visitors hosts or speakers who add to the show. It as a rule begins with an editorial or speech from the host and afterward moves into a board conversation, meeting, or commitment from another source.

A perfect representation is the New Yorker's digital recording named The Writer's Voice.

The Writer's Voice

Web recording host: Deborah Trainman

The Writer's Voice permits mainstream authors just as cutting-edge essayists to peruse one of their pieces on the air.

Portrayal Style

The portrayal style varies, contingent upon the story the writer has decided to peruse out loud, which is a connecting with aspect concerning this digital recording. You don't have the foggiest idea what type, style, or creator will manifest on the show, which is an incredible method to keep audience members tuning in every week.

Vocal Qualities of the Podcast Host

Deborah Trainman's voice can be depicted as quieting and mitigating. Since the objective of the webcast is to recount a story, her voice lays everything out for loosening up the listening experience. She talks with a legitimate tone.

Other famous instances of half and half digital recordings:

- Record's the Gist

3. Meetings/Panel Discussion

Another famous style of web recording facilitating is having one host, with either a solitary visitor interviewee or various visitors throughout the show. This digital recording type furnishes audience members with various perspectives and is typically a well-known configuration with political webcasts.

Political Gabfest is a mainstream digital recording that utilizes the board conversation design.

Political Gabfest

Portrayal Style

The style of portrayal is more conversational. Albeit the webcast is separated into various sections, the conversation is substantially more like a discussion you may have with your companions. The snare for the audience is that the organization causes it to feel like you are tuning in on a gathering of companions and their musings on different political issues.

Vocal Qualities of the Podcast Hosts

There are three hosts of Political Gabfest. The main host is John Dickerson, who generally peruses the beginning introduction and speech. His vocal style is like a radio commentator, on account of his directing tone. Indeed, his voice makes him the ideal arbitrator of the board conversation, and all through each show, he's ready to take the discussion back to the first thought, if it begins to float. The other two hosts, David Plots and Emily Baseline, both have novel and idiosyncratic voices that make them effectively relatable and simple to tune in to.

Other famous instances of board conversation web recordings:

- The Bean cast

4. Repurposed Content

Repurposing content is another famous approach to collecting your webcast. The substance accessible in 'repurposed style' digital broadcasts goes from classes, workshops, different meetings, and so on, and can truly serve to upgrade the audience members' experience.

A well-known illustration of a digital recording type that utilizes repurposed content is The Moth.

The Moth

Every week, the web recording highlights the best stories that have been told on stages from everywhere in the United States. The Moth can gather these accounts because the tales and sound records are presented by The Moth's audience members. Themes range from individual and social encounters, just as other socially applicable stories.

Portrayal Style

The storyteller is likewise the crowd – every individual who gets up in front of an audience to recount their one of a kind story is an audience of The Moth. Along these lines, the digital recording does an undeniable occupation at making human associations between the audience members and the speakers on the webcast. This kind of digital broadcast is an extraordinary method to connect with and snare audience members.

Other mainstream instances of repurposed content digital recordings:

- The TED
- Radio Hour

Kinds of Podcasts – Which Style Is Right For You?

Since you know a couple of the sorts of digital recordings that are accessible you can begin to settle on a more educated choice on what kind of webcast style and arrangement will suit the ultimate objective of your webcast. Is it accurate to say that you are attempting to illuminate? Pleasure? Engage? Contingent upon your answer, the arrangement will change and the kind of voice you need to embrace will change also.

The most ideal approach to conclude is to tune in to as many digital recordings as you can and figure out the configuration, the host's vocal characteristics, and the style wherein they are introducing data.

Upbeat podcasting!

The Rising Popularity of Podcasting, and Why You're Business Should Care

Digital broadcasts have been causing a considerable amount of commotion recently.

Truly, in a real sense.

For those new to the web recording scene, digital broadcasts are a progression of sound documents made accessible on the web. Most webcasts are set up like a TV or public broadcast, with various "seasons" and scenes zeroed in on changed subjects highlighting uncommon visitors. Audience members can buy into explicit web recordings, download new scenes, and listen to whatever point it's advantageous to them.

While web recordings have been around for about 10 years — recollect 2004 when Apple's iPod minis were extremely popular, and iTunes Music Store had quite recently gone global — there's been a flood in listenership in the last couple of years that is getting a great deal of consideration from entrepreneurs, superstars, promoters, and buyers the same.

How about we investigate six reasons why the rising prominence of pod recordings could matter for your business:

1. It doesn't take a lot to begin.

Something that makes digital recordings so convincing for organizations — particularly organizations with more modest staffs and restricted financial plans — is that they don't need a critical venture to begin. Something as straightforward as recording on a cell phone or tablet ought to be ideal for your initial not many scenes.

Since digital recordings are likewise extremely conversational, you will not have to work out all that you need to say. You can make a diagram early to help you stay on point, yet the greater part of the discussion will be fine unscripted.

2. Web recordings are ideal for narrating.

As a private company, your accounts are what help you attract individuals, get them to put resources into your business, and convince them to pick your business over the opposition. Ideally, you're now searching for ways to carry your one of a kind stories to your online presence like your site, blog, web-based media, and email promoting messages.

Provided that this is true, you're presumably pondering — what's the advantage of adding a webcast to this rundown?

As a sound-based stage, webcasts permit you to bridle more correspondence power than composed words alone. Your audience members will be hearing your accounts directly from the source, as opposed to perusing the words and deciphering them all alone. This will assist you with passing on tone, timing, humor, and fervor in a way that even the most skilled essayist's battle to get across on a page.

3. They're incredibly helpful to burn-through.

More than blog entries or recordings, which request somebody's complete consideration, digital broadcasts give audience members the endowment of performing multiple tasks.

That is the reason most digital recording audience members tune in to webcasts through their cell phones, tablets, or other cell phones. Audience members can tune in to digital recordings while preparing toward the beginning of the day, heading to work, or preparing supper. Digital recording fans can without much of a stretch consolidate listening time into their day by day schedules, which is likely why one of every five-week by week webcast clients burn-through at least six digital broadcasts seven days.

4. You can turn into an industry master.

What sorts of enterprises are utilizing digital recordings? A snappy examination of iTunes will show you everything from sewing to make lager to financial aspects are largely reasonable game.

Consider your ability and crowd, and what subjects you could cover on a continuous premise. Recall that webcasts likewise function admirably for interviews, so you don't need to stress over being the master on each theme you need to cover. You likewise shouldn't be worried about your mastery being to specialty; indeed, specialty webcasts may function admirably because you have less commotion to battle through. You could likewise make some simpler memories of being included on a stage like iTunes if there are fewer digital recordings zeroed in on your particular subject.

5. Your audience members are in it for the long stretch.

Consider the time contrast between an individual from your crowd seeing one of your tweets as opposed to tuning in to a webcast. Digital recordings give your audience members the time they need to get comfortable and connect all the more profoundly with what you're saying.

While the length of digital broadcast scenes differs a considerable amount, holding scenes to 15 - 30 minutes improves the probability that audience members can devour full scenes without interference. Past the time venture, web recordings rouse faithfulness since audience members are becoming acquainted with and trust you. This will move expected clients through the purchasing cycle all the more rapidly and give you the freedom to keep them refreshed on your business' contributions.

6. You can contact another, directed crowd.

Your business is most likely previously considering how to upgrade your site to get found through web indexes. Beginning a web recording will open up promising circumstances for getting found on stages like iTunes, which has 800 million records, or Sound Cloud, with more than 250 million dynamic clients.

New audience members who run over your web recording are frequently the individuals who are looking out for data on a particular subject. This guarantees you're contacting them with the perfect data at the perfect time.

Moreover, you can add buy-in catches to your email bulletins and site to draw in the individuals who are now acquainted with your business.

Prepared to plunge your toes into the webcast stream?

Regardless of whether beginning a web recording claims to you, you may feel uncertain about taking on another responsibility.

Think about making these little strides first:

Tune in to what's out there: Find out what's as of now being made and think about how your methodology would analyze. You can discover late scenes of our new webcast, Small Biz Stories here.

Show up on existing shows: If beginning your webcast isn't sensible for you at present, you can in any case profit by podcasting as a highlighted visitor on existing web recordings. Invest some energy exploring famous digital recordings identified with your industry. Ask clients what webcasts they tune in to. When you find web recordings that could apply to your industry, or that you figure you could enhance, search for freedoms to assemble associations with the hosts. If you have your substance that you think they'll discover intriguing, share it with them so they can see the sort of significant worth you could offer.

CHAPTER EIGHT

Best Podcast Equipment (For Beginners and Pros)

Webcast recording hardware can be confounding to swim through and pick in case you're simply beginning. There is a great deal of web recording gear you can get however that doesn't mean you need to get everything – and you can generally grow your rundown of webcast hardware over the long run.

We will feature the sound account hardware you will require, just as certain things you might need to get later as you get more genuine to truly work out a total digital recording studio. There are isolated posts about a significant number of these individual things, so don't hesitate to look at those posts for additional top to bottom data (there will be a connection in the separate segments).

The fundamental digital recording gear you will require in 2021 are:

- A PC
- A receiver

They are the initial two things recorded underneath. On the off chance that you have various individuals recording together, you will need to dodge USB mica, which implies you'll likewise require a sound interface or blender to connect different XLR receivers. Additionally, investigate the podcasting starter unit for more explicit gear proposals relying upon the number of hosts you have. There are lower-spending alternatives for amateurs, alongside overhauls for moderate and genius levels.

Rundown of Podcasting Gear

- PC
- Sound Interface
- Blender
- Pop Filter/Windscreen
- Earphones
- Earphone Amplifier
- Mic Stands
- Stun Mount
- Receiver Cables
- Acoustic Treatment
- Altering Software (DAW)
- Webcast Hosting
- Site Hosting
- Portable Podcasting Gear
- Advanced Recorder
- Receiver
- SD Card

PC

Sound judgment right? You need a PC to record and transfer your .mp3 documents. A great many people will do fine and dandy with what they have, yet on the off chance that you hoping to update I would put resources into something that will last you a couple of years.

Mouthpiece

Try not to utilize your PC's inherent mouthpiece. The simplest method to begin is to utilize a USB receiver. If you have various individuals or you need greater adaptability, you will require at least one receivers with an XLR yield. Likewise think about your chronicle climate and the kind of mic you'll need: dynamic or condenser (dynamic mic are regularly better when recording various individuals together).

Sound Interface

This is fundamentally the extension between your receiver and your PC. It changes over the simple sign from the mic into a computerized signal that the PC can utilize.

Blender

Comparable to the sound interface above, however, a blender gives you more power over levels, data sources, yields, and that's only the tip of the iceberg. Additionally essential if you plan to routinely have brought in visitors so you get set up a blend short line for your far off visitors.

Pop Filter/Windscreen

A pop channel or windscreen will incredibly limit or forestall plosives. Put your hand before your mouth and say "power" – feel the air on the "p"? That is the thing that you're shielding the mic from – those air impacts can without much of a stretch send a mic into the red.

Earphones

Earphones forestall numerous errors and retakes. It tends to be bizarre to hear yourself talking live from the start, yet you'll become acclimated to it. It's strongly prescribed you become acclimated to this. You would prefer not to record something for an hour just to acknowledge something wasn't turned on or there was an uproarious buzz the entire time.

Shut back earphones are what you need to use for recording, and your ear buds presumably aren't sufficient. Dodge open-back earphones for recording because your amplifier will get the sound.

Earphone Amplifier

At the point when you have a few hosts, you'll need an earphone amp with the goal that every one of you can have your pair of earphones. Consider it an earphone splitter and speaker in one.

Mic Stands

Situating your mouthpiece appropriately will incredibly improve your stance and sound quality. A nice blast arm or mic stand will permit you to effectively move the mouthpiece to an agreeable position – and similarly significant in my brain, you'll have the option to let lose work area space and store the mic reachable, however out the way when you're not utilizing it.

Stun Mount

Mouthpieces are particularly touchy to any solid that doesn't need to go through the air. A stun mount will forestall or limit undesirable sounds from tapping the work area to composing to moving your blast arm to little vibrations that you probably won't take note of. Most amplifier producers additionally offer a viable stun mount, and some even furnish one with the mic.

Amplifier Cables

You need to plug your mic into your sound interface, blender, or preamp in one way or another.

There is in reality a great deal that goes into XLR mouthpiece links and modest ones can mess more up than they're worth.

Acoustic Treatment

A few rooms are more awful than others, yet if your account zone has a great deal of reverberation or reverb, a little acoustic treatment can go far.

Altering Software (DAW)

For amateurs, the digital recording altering programming I suggest is Audacity or Garage band. They're both free and moderately simple to utilize and learn. The following level up is Adobe Audition, and on the off chance that you as of now have a Creative Cloud membership, it's presumably a smart thought to simply go with that.

Webcast Hosting

You need to be devoted to facilitating your digital recording documents (I utilize and suggest Buzz sprout).

It's a typical confusion, however, iTunes doesn't have your genuine .mp3 records, they just read an RSS channel and permit individuals to play your documents facilitated somewhere else. Figure out how to transfer to iTunes here. You would prefer not to put the documents on your site have because that can without much of a stretch make your site go to a slither, and can cause issues when individuals attempt to tune in.

Site Hosting

Many digital broadcasts will require a site to give individuals a spot to visit, find out additional, and get extra assets.

I suggest utilizing a Word Press facilitating administration.

One of the least demanding to begin with is Blue host and they have an incredible evaluation for new locales.

Computerized Recorder

In case you're doing interviews out and about, a convenient advanced recorder will be your closest companion. You can generally begin with an outside mic for your iPhone, however, a committed handheld recorder will give you much greater adaptability (they can even serve as a USB interface).

Receiver

Many choices are relying upon the style of web recording you will do. In case you're talking with individuals, look at these meeting receivers.

SD Card

Remember the additional capacity for your advanced recorder! Snatch a couple of these SanDisk 32GB cards so you don't run out of space out and about. Make certain to twofold check what the maximum SD card size will work for your recorder (the H4N Pro above permits up to 32GB).

Podcast Recording Equipment

Record utilizing sound programming

In case you're facilitating your show solo, this will be the least demanding approach to record your digital broadcast. Why? Since all you require is a USB mic and your #1 altering program. Setting up is pretty much as straightforward as connecting your mouthpiece, ensuring it's chosen in sound inclinations, and hitting record. The one thing you must be cautious about, nonetheless, is the place where you record. In case you're setting up a home studio your chronicle space should be sound amicable. That implies staying away from rooms with intelligent surfaces like tiles, windows, or high roofs. You don't have to go through a great deal of cash getting this right. Indeed, a couple of thick drapes or sofa pads will do. In any case, you need to place thought into the nature of sound when you're recording on the off chance that you need your show to be a triumph.

Adobe Audition

A membership program I use to alter all my digital broadcasts. It's utilized by experts however it's not as scary as possible still effectively understand it in case you're an amateur.

Record utilizing Skype

This is one approach to record when you have visitors on your show or co-has who aren't in a similar area. Once more, you simply need a PC and an amplifier however you'll be recording through Skype as opposed to sound altering programming. Customarily you needed to download extra projects to do this yet Skype has as of late added a chronicle alternative to its most recent form. It's essential to note, in any case, that correct now you can just record Skype to Skype calls utilizing this component not Skype to calls. I use call recording programming since I'm utilized to it and I like the usefulness. So if you need to attempt that technique the projects I suggest are Encamp (for Mac) and Pamela (for PC). Skype is extraordinary because you can see your visitor however you can likewise utilize it to call individuals on the telephone which can give greater adaptability as far as who you can get on your show. Simply be careful the sound nature of somebody on the telephone is lower than different strategies for recording so you shouldn't utilize this constantly if there's anything you can do about it.

Record utilizing Zen caster or Ringer

With both Zen caster and Ringer you welcome visitors to join a meeting and every individual's sound is recorded locally then put something aside for you to utilize later. This implies you end up with two top-notch records you can sort out to make it sound like you were in a similar area. The lone restriction with this technique is you can't see each other so a simple fix is to run Skype all the while (with your PC misc. quieted so you don't hear screechy criticism). It's additionally critical to ensure you're someplace with a solid web association, in any case, the sound can exist among you and your visitor. This will not influence the actual chronicle yet it can genuinely affect the beat of discussion.

Record utilizing a versatile account gadget

This is the thing that I recommend in case you're intending to record face to face with individuals and need to convey hardware with you. My top proposal for this is the Zoom H6. It's the gadget I use to record all my web recordings and its compact and dependable... simply make sure to pack extra batteries or you'll be reviling yourself.

Record utilizing Anchor

There are upsides and downsides to this application because while I'm supportive of making podcasting simpler I don't feel that should come to the detriment of value. As somebody who's utilized to more granular altering programming, I discovered Anchor didn't give me as much adaptability as I required in alters. Yet, you may be a flat out a firearm at this program and feel like it's the most ideal alternative for you to make something that sounds incredible.

What do you need to start a podcast?

To begin a digital broadcast, at an absolute minimum, you need to:

- Think of an idea (a theme, name, organization, and target length for every scene).
- Plan craftsmanship and compose a portrayal to "brand" your webcast.
- Record and alter your sound documents, (for example, MP3s). An amplifier is suggested (more on digital broadcast hardware later).
- Discover a spot to have your records, (for example, a document have that spends significant time in webcasts, as Lipson or Pod bean).
- Partner these sound records into an RSS channel so they can be dispersed through Apple Podcasts and downloaded or spilled on any gadget on-request.

Recording and editing Your Podcast

Instructions to record a webcast

About how to record a digital broadcast, you should simply connect a USB receiver and open the sound account programming on your PC. Guarantee your receiver is connected and turned on and that your mouthpiece is the default input gadget for your account programming. Click the record button in your product of decision and talk away! There's no compelling reason to stop or interruption the chronicle, regardless of whether there are botches en route. You can generally alter the chronicle later utilizing similar programming. To record your first scene in Garage Band, here's a decent four-minute video that will handily walk you through the interaction: When you complete the process of recording, you'll need to save your webcast. MP3s are the best configuration for your web recording documents since they pack well (low record size) and can be played on most gadgets. You'll need to save your MP3 as a fixed bitrate and not a variable (VBR) one. Most chronicle programming will ask you for this data after saving. A decent bitrate to utilize is 128kbps, which keeps the record size low while keeping up the great sound quality. For the example rate, I suggest 44.1 MHz, which is CD quality.

1. What Are the Podcast Editing "Rules"?

Right off the bat, however, I referenced that there's no single way you "ought to" be altering your digital broadcast. Surely, there are acceptable and terrible practices, yet its altogether up to you if you even alter your show by any stretch of the imagination. If you need to make an exceptionally delivered digital recording or sound dramatization, at that point, somehow, that will require a reasonable piece of altering. However, in case you're simply recording yourself talking into a mic, and don't feel the requirement for any introduction music, at that point you can pull off no altering by any means.

2. Would it be a good idea for me to Use a DAW for My Podcast Editing?

The most widely recognized web recording altering device is the thing that's known as a DAW – that represents Digital Audio Workstation. It's simply a luxurious method of saying "sound altering program". DAWs likewise let you record into them, so it's fundamentally similar to having a full account studio on your PC – giving you have a receiver to plug into it. The most famous fledgling DAW is one called Audacity. It's famous because it's free. It's even more than adequate to construct your digital recording scene. However, in case you're searching for an all the more supportive of level DAW with a practically limitless number of capacities and abilities, at that point Adobe Audition or Reaper may be more up your road. Beneath, you'll locate our full correlation among Audacity and Audition which will ideally assist you with choosing which one (assuming any) you'd like to utilize. Also, on the off chance that you're hoping to adopt both of them rapidly and ably, at that point we have video seminars on both inside The Podcast Host Academy.

3. Shouldn't something be said about Podcast Editing Apps and Tools?

Digital broadcast altering is the most well-known thing we're gotten some information about here at The Podcast Host. That prompted us to build up a device called Alito, which constructs your scene for you. It can deal with the handling, altering, and distributing of your digital broadcast, without the requirement for a DAW. This is a truly easy to-utilize apparatus focused on "non-nerd" individuals. Complete amateurs, and podcasters who essentially don't have the opportunity to spend altering their webcasts more customarily. There are some other extraordinary applications out there as well. Most importantly, nowadays, you needn't bother with a DAW to alter your web recording. Truth be told, you can web record while never having opened one in your life.

4. Would it be a good idea for me to hire a Producer to Do My Podcast Editing?

Still, got no interest in having anything to do with your web recording altering? That is entirely typical. It simply implies that you'll most likely need to enlist somebody to do it for you. There are a steadily developing number of makers out there who make themselves accessible for webcast altering work. These reach from specialists with day occupations, to completely fledged organizations utilizing groups of web recording makers on their staff. The course you go down will, as could be, rely upon your spending plan. You'll discover heaps of incredible consultants out there accomplishing extraordinary work with ease. In any case, similar to some other assistance, there will without a doubt be a couple of questionable people in the commercial center as well.

Recruiting a Producer: Options

Music Radio Creative will give you a moment quote dependent on your normal scene length and the measure of scenes you'd prefer to focus on. We take on some creative work ourselves here at The Podcast Host. We much of the time work with customers to dispatch their digital broadcasts through a progression of training and coaching meetings. At that point, we'll assume the underlying altering of their scenes whenever they've been recorded. You can discover more about our digital recording creation administration here.

Digital recording Editing Software

No two digital recordings are indistinguishable (that is completely false, there are at any rate 500 "business person" shows with the words

"On Fire" in their title, yet we'll brush past that!), so this all descends to your one of a kind methodology, and points.

For the Hobbyist or "Toe-Dipper"

In case you're a specialist who's simply hoping to talk about a point near your heart, at that point setting aside some effort to become familiar with the rudiments of Audacity is presumably the most ideal alternative for you. Keep in mind, on the off chance that you'd prefer to take a seminar on Audacity (or Audition) at that point you can do that inside The Podcast Host Academy.

For the Small Business or Side-Hustle

In case you're somebody at present working normal employment, except dispatching your show as a feature of a side business that you're not kidding about developing, at that point you may be set up to go through a minimal expenditure to save money on schedule. All things considered, utilizing the "web recording making" application Alito is presumably your most ideal alternative.

For the Company or Brand Podcast

Or on the other hand, in case you're a set-up business hoping to get a profoundly cleaned and proficient sounding show directly out the door, at that point recruiting a maker will be your most ideal alternative. Simply recollect that extraordinary sounding sound is more to do with the source material than the altering, however, so employ somebody who can prompt you on your chronicle arrangement and work with you on that front as well.

Sound chronicle programming

The product suggested in this part will permit you to record the sound from your amplifier and save it as an MP3 document. The accompanying programming will likewise permit you to alter your accounts, which I'll go over in more detail later in this guide.

Sound Recording Software

Adobe Audition (PC/Mac; USD 20.99 each month): If you need truly amazing sound altering programming with all the fancy odds and ends, Adobe has it with Audition. It very well may be an excess to alter your webcast, yet in case you're utilizing a blender and top of the line gear, it very well may be a smart thought to view at Adobe Audition too. Boldness (PC/Mac; Free): An audacity is an extraordinary option in contrast to paid, premium sound altering programming. It's not difficult to utilize and there is a lot of instructional exercises accessible online to assist you with figuring out how to utilize them. Garage Band (Mac; Free): Garage Band accompanies all MacBook's and is adequate for the greater part of your sound altering needs. Garage Band permits you to record the sound from your digital broadcast mouthpiece and save it as an MP3.

Call recording programming

If you plan on leading meetings for your webcast, you should utilize programming that records your calls. In case you're utilizing a blender that records all stable from your PC, this product will not be needed. Nonetheless, in case you're utilizing an essential arrangement and an instrument like Skype or Google Hangouts to direct meetings, here are some suggested call recording apparatuses:

Zen caster (PC/Mac; allowed to begin). Record far off meetings in studio quality by sending a connection and accepting a track for every visitor.

Encamp Call Recorder (Mac; $39.95 USD). Record Skype approaches your Mac. Uber Conference (PC/Mac/iOS/Android; free). The free phone call programming permits members to join the call through the work area or telephone, and the arbitrator can record the calls. Call note (PC/Mac; free to USD 9.95 each year). Call note records Skype, Google Hangouts, and Viber, Face Time, Facebook, GoToMeeting, and WebEx discussions.

Recording podcast interviews

Interview Your Podcast Guests Remotely

By Natalie Jones

Step by step instructions to record visitors distantly is quite possibly the most well-known inquiries new podcasters and sound makers pose. You will seldom have the financial plan or an opportunity to report a story or scene precisely how you need it. There is minimal possibility of flying around to talk with every one of your sources, to guarantee predictable, top-notch sound. Luckily, innovation has given us a few ways to deal with far off chronicle. You can in any case record excellent sound without being there with your visitor.

Work Out Your Set-Up

If you are as of now working in sound, apparently you have an approach to record yourself and others face to face. This may be your compact recorder, for example, those made by Zoom, Tascam, or Marantz (preferably with an outside mouthpiece), or perhaps it's a USB mic connected to your PC. Whichever it is, utilize the best accessible choice while talking with somebody distantly.

You should get a mic stand, on the off chance that you don't as of now have one, so you don't have to hold the mic all through your whole discussion. Regardless of whether your finish of the discussion isn't being recorded in a similar spot or a similar configuration as the interviewee's, you can match up to them later, and it's ideal to get the greatest sound you can.

Set Your Guest Up for Success

Above all else, your interviewee will require a peaceful life with an entryway that closes where they can do the meeting. The best rooms are little, with low roofs and whatever number of extravagant surfaces as could be allowed—floor coverings, shades, and delicate furnishings.

Then, sort out how you'll be chatting with them. Do they have a landline (uncommon), a PDA, as well as a PC with a web association in that room? Possibly an outside receiver? The choice you pick pushing ahead relies upon your interviewee's circumstance.

Alternative A: Quiet Room + Computer with Internet Connection (Best)

+ External USB Mic

In the most ideal situation, your interviewee has a PC with a web association and an outside USB mic. On the off chance that they do, at that point, those are ideal for them to utilize.

+ Headphones/Ear buds with Mic

It is likely your interviewee will not have an outside mic, and that is fine. If they have a headset with a little receiver or a couple of ear buds, request that they utilize that.

+ Internal Computer Mic

Then again, they can utilize the inner receiver on their PC, however, this is the most un-alluring choice as it will get a ton of commotion in the room—attempt to keep away from that. Make a record with a web recording administration—Zen caster and Squad cast are two of the most very much respected. (Valuing changes for these, however, the two of them have reasonable choices.) With these administrations, you can set up an arrangement for your discussion, much the same as setting up a gathering. Your guest(s) will just have to click connect to join the gathering. At the point when you wrap up talking, their sound (just as yours) will naturally be accessible to download as separate tracks. Note: this choice necessitates that the visitor has sufficient free space on their PC to record the sound.

Skype and Zoom additionally have recording choices, yet those administrations are recording the actual association, not the voices coming into the PC's equipment, so the sound quality won't be pretty much as great as on something like Zen caster or Squad cast.

+ Smartphone as Mic

On the off chance that your interviewee doesn't have an outer mouthpiece however has a cell phone, they can utilize their cell phone as an outside mic. Direct your meeting utilizing a help like Skype or Zoom, and have them record themselves with their cell phone. If they have an iPhone, the voice reminder application that comes standard functions admirably. If they have an Android, they can download a voice-recording application like Easy Voice Recorder or ASR Voice Recorder.

The drawback of this choice is that it requires the visitor to send the record to you after the meeting. While this is certainly not a convoluted interaction, it very well may be interesting for less technically knowledgeable visitors, and can here and there raise a ruckus if the record is truly enormous. (You might need to stop the meeting in the center to begin another document, to help forestall huge record issues.)

It can likewise be nerve-wracking to put the onus of conveying the document all on your visitor—you might need to have a back-up account in this situation. The telephone additionally needs to remain very near to the individual's mouth with this strategy; you might need to request the visitor to make remain from some sort—a pinnacle of books functions admirably—to lay the telephone on and bring it up higher. They could likewise hold it all through the whole meeting, however, this may get tiring and increment taking care of commotion. Aspen Public Radio made this extraordinary video disclosing the cycle to visitors—it's a couple of years old, yet at the same time supportive.

Choice B: Quiet Room + Smartphone (Okay)

On the off chance that the interviewee just has a cell phone accessible, yet doesn't have a PC and web association, there are applications intended for this situation. Ringer works comparably to Zen caster and Squad cast in that it utilizes the telephone's receiver, not simply the telephone association, to record the individual talking, and afterward makes the document accessible to you to download straightforwardly after the call. Yet, it requires the visitor to download the application onto their telephone before the meeting and leave it open toward the end while the document is transferring. Simply adhere to Ringer's directions to set up a call, and have your visitor click the welcome connection that comes to them to join the call. Other comparable administrations we have not tried are Clear cast and Cast.

The guidelines for the alternative underneath will likewise work for this situation.

Choice C: Quiet Room + Landline or (Non-Smartphone) Cell Phone

In the present circumstance, you might need to make a decent attempt as you can to reschedule or discover different choices for your visitor that is not generally conceivable, and this might be their lone accessible set-up. For this situation, you can utilize an application on your telephone that records the actual call (instead of utilizing the telephone's inherent mouthpiece) to record your discussion. Tape Call is mainstream for the iPhone, and Another Call Recorder is a famous Android variant. The sound quality will be lower with these—it will sound more like the "telephone tape" that you once in a while hear on the radio and in digital recordings, and isn't prescribed if you intend to utilize long parts in your last delivery or broadcast. Another detriment of these choices is that they don't record every individual on a different track, which decreases your adaptability when altering. These administrations are truly intended for individuals who simply need the recorded sound as a source of perspective, however not for broadcast. One significant bit of leeway, however, is that your visitor doesn't have to do anything on their finish to make it work—the applications will send you the sound.

Long haul Option: Serial or "Radio Diaries"

You intend to meet your visitor a few times throughout an extensive period or need them to record "radio journals" all alone. With this sort of announcing the plan, you might need to think about purchasing a basic recorder and sending it to your visitor, with a snappy instructional exercise on the most proficient method to utilize it. A few recorders that function admirably for this are the Zoom H1N and the Tascam-DRO5. For educated visitors, you might have the option to mentor them on transferring the records to a PC and sending them to you. On the other hand, simply have them mail the whole recorder back to you when they're set. The conspicuous downsides of this methodology are your dependence on the visitor, and the time delay between when the sound is recorded and when you have it.

High Production Budget Option: Tape Snyder

On the off chance that you can manage the cost of it, the most ideal approach to distant chronicle is to employ what's referred to in the business as a "Tape Snyder." This is an expert records who lives in your visitor's territory and will go meet your visitor at their home or office. They'll hold a great amplifier associated with an advanced recorder up to them while they chat on the telephone with you, at that point send you the documents subsequently. The standard rate for these positions is about $150 per meeting, in addition to mileage, for a meeting of about 1.5 hours or less.

You can discover a Tape Snyder through organizations, for example, the Association of Independents in Radio (which requires an enrollment charge to join and look through the organization), or other nearby sound organizations or lusters. You could likewise give arriving at a shot to columnists at the nearby open radio broadcast in your visitor's region—regularly those correspondents are keen on doing tape synchronizes, or know another person who is. With this methodology, you'll get proficient sound quality on the two sides of the discussion (accepting that you're additionally recording yourself with proficient staff), and the nearest you can get to studio-quality without going to a studio.

Sync + Edit

Recording worked out in a good way, and now you have all the sound. It's an ideal opportunity to match up to it up and begin altering.

Ideally, you have at any rate two separate sound documents, one for your side of the discussion and one for your guests. (Or then again more, on the off chance that you had more than one visitor.) You'll need to open them both in whatever sound altering program you're utilizing (some of the time called a computerized sound workstation—DAW); Protocol's, Audition, Hindenburg, and Reaper are famous with sound makers. With a portion of these techniques (utilizing Zen caster, Squad cast, or Ringer) the sound will as of now be a similar length and matched up appropriately because you began and finished the accounts simultaneously. With others, your records may be marginally various lengths and start and stop at various occasions. You'll have to coordinate the different sides of the discussion with one another, which can be precarious. One approach to assist with this is to make a bad quality reinforcement recording of the call with some other framework—for example in case you're recording with mouthpieces on one or the flip side, yet talking over Skype, you can have Skype record the call. At that point.

CHAPTER NINE

PODCAST ARTWORK

Your web recording cover craftsmanship is the primary experience potential audience members have with your show as they peruse on Apple Podcasts, Google Podcasts, Spottily, or their most loved digital broadcast application. They'll utilize your work of art to choose if they should peruse your portrayal, skim your scene titles, or tune in to their first scene making it a basic piece of advancing your webcast. Although you didn't persuade into podcasting to be a craftsman, you need to pay attention to your webcast cover workmanship. Ahead, we'll turn out how to make quality webcast symbolism that develops your show.

Web recording Cover Art Requirements for Apple Podcasts and Spottily

To start with, we should discuss the specialized stuff. Ensure you are web recording cover workmanship meets this model absolutely for the greatest permeability. If it doesn't, the web recording indexes may neglect to show your picture or decline to show your show altogether.

- Your web recording craftsmanship ought to be square. Make it 3000 pixels by 3000 pixels. This way it will look great all over, in any event, when downsized. 1400 pixels by 1400 pixels is the base for Apple Podcasts.
- Make it 72 dpi and use RGB tones.
- Save your specialty as a JPEG or PNG (yet JPEG is ideal).
- Regardless of whether they're inside the above details, Pod news as of late found work of art filenames with more than

one period, as coverart.001.jpeg, will bomb the Apple Podcasts approval measure.

- Ensure your craftsmanship conforms to Apple's prerequisites before submitting it to Apple Podcasts. Survey their documentation here.
- Before submitting to spottily, peruse their conveyance particulars to ensure you're consistent. Audit their documentation here.

Tips for Podcast Cover Art and Logos

Since you comprehend the specialized models, you need to realize how to plan a satisfying and alluring picture. These aren't firm principles, yet they're acceptable tips to help make your webcast cover craftsmanship appealing, drawing in, and justifiable.

1. Leave some space among words and the edges of the picture

Do whatever it takes not to pack the picture with content. Give it some space to breathe. This will likewise assist audience members with understanding your craftsmanship regardless of whether the digital broadcast player or index cuts off a piece of it.

2. View your fine art when it's little

Some applications and players will scale your picture as little as 30 pixels by 30 pixels, so review it at that size to ensure individuals will get it.

3. Try not to utilize multiple text styles

Utilize one text style for your digital recording's title and another textual style for the subheading (on the off chance that you have one). Any more is diverting and chaotic. Great Night Stories for Rebel Girls is a lively show about unprecedented ladies. Its cover craftsmanship communicates the show's topics of experience and going after greater things with extraordinary text styles and tempting tones.

4. Try not to utilize senseless, difficult to-peruse, or gimmicky text styles

It's alright to display your character, yet you would prefer not to be hard to comprehend. In particular, ensure your text styles are not difficult to peruse. You don't need somebody to look past your show since they can't peruse its title. This webcast cover craftsmanship for Inside Psycho is about clear typography. You can promptly tell that this will be a spooky show that plunges into a disrupting subject, however, it's still simple to peruse.

5. Recount a sharp story

Utilize your cover craftsmanship to communicate the center subject of your digital recording. You may need to recruit a craftsman or planner to make the ideal picture, however, it will worth the cash on the off chance that it pulls in new audience members. For instance, the Strangers digital broadcast utilizes a picture that encourages you to comprehend what is the issue here.

6. Cutoff the number of words you use

Your work of art should be comprehensible in little sizes, so don't attempt to pack in a passage (or even a long sentence). Utilize your show's name as the principal feature. Subheadings are alright, yet keep them short and punchy. Record's Slow Burn doesn't mess with a lot of words. It just utilizes the webcast's title and the brand name. It allows the exceptionally conspicuous picture to accomplish all the work.

7. Avoid abused pictures like amplifiers or headsets

Receivers, headsets, and different pictures identifying with podcasting are platitude now. Keep away from them if you can, regardless of whether your show is tied in with podcasting. Else you will not stick out. S-Town is a story webcast about a shameful town in Alabama. The cover workmanship utilizes eye-getting shadings and extraordinary symbolism. You don't typically see blossoms and timekeepers together like that, so it makes you can't help thinking about what is the issue here.

8. Make your cover fine art predictable with the remainder of your marking

Utilize a similar duplicate, pictures, text styles, and shadings. The objective is to make a predictable vibe across your whole image, regardless of where your fans collaborate with you. This causes them to make an association with you.

9. Try not to be hesitant to utilize your logo

On the off chance that your web recording is essential for a bigger association that individuals as of now perceive, your digital broadcast cover workmanship should use that marking. Notice how Nike remembers their switch logo for the entirety of their webcast craftsmanship.

10. Utilize high-goal pictures

Since your cover workmanship will ordinarily be shown little, you need it to be pretty much as clear as could be expected. If your digital broadcast cover is grainy, foggy, or slanted to odd extents, potential audience members will scroll directly by it. They will accept your helpless cover craftsmanship is an impression of your show's helpless creation esteem.

11. Pick differentiating colors

Striking tones encourage you to stand apart from the group, particularly if your shadings are lively and eye-getting. Notice how these cover pictures jump out at you since they utilize differentiating blacks, grays, whites, and yellows.

NEWS & POLITICS
Embedded

SOCIETY & CULTURE
**It's Been a Minute
with Sam Sanders**

BUSINESS
**How I Built This
with Guy Raz**

12. Try not to swarm your web recording cover workmanship with a lot of substance

The void area is a basic component of any plan, so don't swarm your picture's components. We love this digital recording cover workmanship due to its clear, attractive tones, however, it isn't packed with complex pictures or text. The tones and the appearance on the lady's face make it stick out.

13. Make your cover picture flexible for different mediums

For example, you should utilize your cover craftsmanship to advance on Facebook, as a static picture when you republish on YouTube, or as some piece of your web recording site. Consider the components of these areas as you plan your picture.

14. Evade express or grown-up just pictures and language

These things either disregard the particulars of the large web recording registries or potentially dismiss individuals from your show.

- References to drugs, sex, gore, foulness, savagery, or disdain topics.
- Pictures or dialects that reference bigotry, homophobia, or sexism.
- Complex words that the vast majority will not comprehend.

15. Evade words pictures that are the protected innovation of different brands

These disregard the standards of most webcast chiefs. Utilizing another person's property can likewise push you in a great deal of difficulty (except if you have the authorization to utilize them).

16. Try not to be reluctant to utilize your face

On the off chance that your crowd knows you well, it very well may be shrewd to utilize your face on your webcast cover craftsmanship. This is Your Life by creator and mentor Michael Hyatt does this well. Likewise, notice how his picture coordinates the marking on his site. Truth be told, Lots of well-known individuals put their appearances on their webcast cover workmanship.

17. Review your cover craftsmanship each across podcasting applications

Ensure your digital recording work of art looks extraordinary before submitting it. Use Podcast Artwork Check to see it on numerous stages. The most effective method to Make Your Podcast Cover Art or Logo. Prepared to cause your own to web recording cover craftsmanship? You have two alternatives here: 1) you can either pay somebody to make it for you utilizing assistance like 99designs or Fiver. 2) Make it yourself utilizing a DIY configuration apparatus like Canvas, Tailor Brands, or Adobe Spark.

99designs (paid)

99 plans is a planning stage that gives you admittance to a large number of gifted fashioners. You essentially mention to them what you need to be planned and employ an architect. You can likewise

open your solicitation to the local area, let creators test out your thoughts, and pick your top choice. Figure out how it functions.

Fiver (paid)

Fiver is another stage for creators. You need to discover the creator that is ideal for your necessities, however, it's altogether less expensive than most plan administrations. Quest for fashioners who offer gigs explicitly for webcast craftsmanship (or simply click here). Figure out how it functions.

Canvas (DIY)

Canvas is a self-administration configuration device that is it's not difficult to utilize and free. It tends to be utilized to make any sort of fine art, so you'll see it helpful to make online media pictures, diagrams, and graphs, blog entry included pictures, and so on We suggest messing with it for a piece to figure out how it functions. When you pursue Canvas and enter your dashboard, click the Create a Design button, select + Custom Dimensions, and enter 3000 for stature and width. The page that opens is your workspace. This is the place where you'll add photographs and text to make your web recording cover craftsmanship. Try to look at their planned instructional exercises.

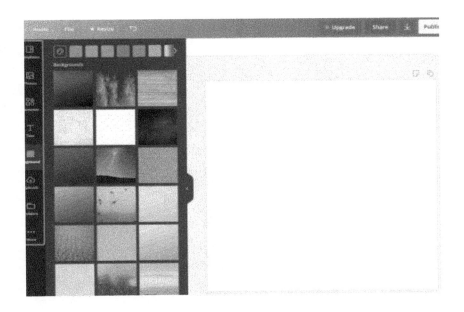

Tailor Brands (DIY)

Tailor Brands is a basic method to make a logo in minutes. Their AI-based framework asks you a couple of inquiries about your favored style and afterward concocts extraordinary fine art only for you. You would then be able to tweak it to ensure it's ideal. Figure out how it functions.

Adobe Spark (DIY)

Adobe Spark is important for the Adobe suite that additionally incorporates Photoshop and Illustrator. In contrast to those high-level devices, Spark is an essential manager that is ideal for unpracticed planners. Their webcast cover workmanship maker is ideal for non-originators who need extraordinary fine art. Making web recording cover craftsmanship is simple: Simply pick one of their expert layouts and add your logo, pictures, and text. Making a cover just requires a couple of moments. Figure out how it functions (look to the base).

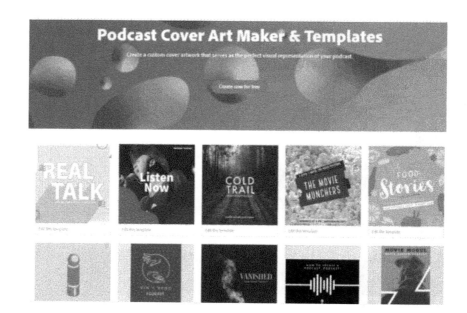

Habitually Asked Questions about Podcast Cover Art

Here are some normal inquiries podcasters pose about their digital recording cover craftsmanship.

Would it be a good idea for me to utilize diverse incognito craftsmanship pictures for every scene?

For the most part, you need consistency with your web recording cover so individuals figure out how to perceive your image. Your logo and slogan should remain the equivalent. In any case, it's okay to roll out certain improvements to keep things new. For example, you may:

- Add the title of the scene
- Add the picture of a prominent visitor to allure audience members.
- Update the cover workmanship for unique scenes to make them stick out (like commemorations, look backs, season finales, and so on)
- Add unique symbolism to assist the crowd with understanding what the issue here is.

- Simply make sure to keep some consistency so audience members can tell initially that the scene is important for your show. You don't need them to believe it's another webcast without fail.

Would I be able to change my digital recording cover picture after my show dispatches?

Truly. As indicated by numerous individuals from Podcast Movement, there aren't any negative impacts of refreshing your cover craftsmanship picture. Your webcast develops after some time thus can your cover craftsmanship. To change your webcast cover craftsmanship in Castors, visit the "feed subtleties" page of your digital broadcast settings.

At that point click "Transfer new picture" to supplant your current picture. This will open the Word Press Media Library.

I changed my webcast cover craftsmanship however it's not refreshing in Apple Podcasts. Why?

To start with, ensure the new cover workmanship has an alternate document name the one you're supplanting and that it meets Apple's picture limitations. Sit tight for 48 hours for it to produce results. If it doesn't show up following two days, contact podcastsupport@apple.com and let them know about the issue.

My RSS channel has a blunder on account of my digital broadcast cover craftsmanship picture. How would it be advisable for me to respond?

- If you ran your RSS channel through a web recording validator (like Pod base) and got a blunder, attempt these fixes:
- If the document size is excessively enormous, pack utilizing Squash and recoveries as a JPG (not a PNG).

- If the document is some unacceptable measurements, resize utilizing Canvas or Squash.
- If the document has some unacceptable DPI, convert it utilizing Cleo.

Outline

Your webcast cover workmanship is a basic component of your image. It's the picture audience members see each time they play a scene, and it's the main thing potential audience members see when they look for new substances. If your craftsmanship is exhausting, unsuitable, and like all the other things, potential audience members will not get attempt your show. They'll scroll directly past your name as they search for something energizing. So it's critical to utilize the tips and instruments we disclosed above to plan top-notch digital recording cover craftsmanship for your image. It very well may be the distinction between a major, connected with the crowd, and no crowd by any stretch of the imagination.

CHAPTER TEN

GETTING YOUR PODCAST LISTED

Definitive Podcast Directory List (2020)

When you transfer your digital recording's first scene, getting recorded in all the top webcast registries is the primary thing to get done! Indexes like Apple Podcasts are stages that help individuals find and stream your substance, and except if you list your web recording in the most broadly utilized stages, audience members can't discover your show. By and large, indexes don't have or circulate your digital broadcast — that is up to your web recording host. All things considered, catalogs center generally around giving a brought together spot to digital recording audience members to find new substance. We should separate the nine significant digital broadcast registries you need to move recorded in immediately and work our way down to specialty catalogs that can additionally extend your show's range!

The best web recording catalogs to list your show

Posting your show on the most famous podcasting stages is fundamental for an effective webcast promoting technique. A large portion of your audience members will discover your web recording in one of these nine significant outlets, so we recommend you present your show to everyone.

1. Apple Podcasts (in the past iTunes)

Apple Podcast is the most established, biggest, and generally significant of all the digital broadcast indexes. When you're prepared to dispatch your show, your next occupation is getting recorded in Apple Podcasts. A greater part of digital recording audience members find new substances through Apple Podcasts and utilize the Podcasts application on their iPhones to stream their number one shows.

Podcast Resources.
Let your voice be heard.

2. Spottily

Spottily is perhaps the most well-known webcast catalogs, yet we propose doing some exploration on this stage to ensure it's a solid match for you. Spottily is a music streaming application, so on the off chance that you do choose to list your webcast with them, your show could contact a crowd of people that wouldn't discover you in any case? You'll additionally approach the application's new details highlight to follow your show's exhibition. The index as of late rolled out certain improvements concerning advertisement position, and now utilizes data about its clients to embed promotions into their substance (Streaming Ad Insertion). Spottily is accessible for the two iOS and Android, so audience members can utilize it regardless of what cell phone they use. Get digital recording into spottily.

3. *Google Podcasts*

Google is eliminating Google Play Music and podcasting audience members to move their memberships to Google Podcasts. As they center more on podcasting the registry will probably keep on developing as it contends with significant outlets. Google's web recording registry doesn't have a standard accommodation measure and rather utilizes search innovation to slither the web and discover shows to list in their index. Ensure your digital recording follows Google's rules so it very well may be gotten and recorded in the catalog. If you have your digital recording on Buzz sprout, your webcast site is naturally viable with Google Podcasts. Get recorded in Google Podcasts

4. *Tune in Radio*

Tune in Radio is the default web recording player for Amazon's Alexa gadgets and broadcasts web radio and webcasts to a local area of more than 75 million dynamic clients joined. By and large, Tune In represents a little level of complete web recording tunes in, however, their associations make your show accessible in a couple of extra spots (like Tesla vehicles, for example). Tune In's podcasting application is accessible on android, iOS, Google Home, Car Play, and the sky is the limit from there. Get digital broadcast recorded in Tune in Radio.

5. Stitcher

Stitcher was one of the first-truly podcasting applications for Android clients. It's presently one of the biggest outsider registries on the planet broadcasting music, webcasts, and web radio. Stitcher additionally offers details on your show's presentation with experiences that can assist you with making content. The stage has a huge number of clients and is accessible on iOS, Android, PC, savvy speakers, and incorporated into more than 50 vehicle models. Get digital broadcast recorded in Stitcher.

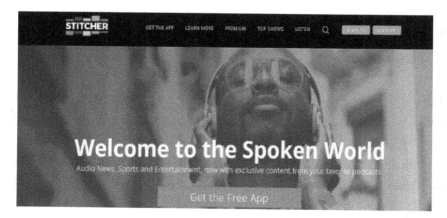

6. Pandora

Pandora's proposal motors are as yet perhaps the most ideal approaches to find new music — and they've as of late made them considerably more remarkable. Pandora as of late refreshed its accommodation cycle to acknowledge a lot more digital recordings, and we're eager to perceive how they influence their rating frameworks to assist audience members with finding shows.

Get digital recording recorded in Pandora.

7. Listen to Notes

Listen Notes is the best digital recording web index out there and capacities like the Google of webcasts. Clients can scan the registry for explicit subjects, and the outcomes frequently grandstand autonomous podcasters who wouldn't show up in an Apple Podcast search. Most podcasters with a public RSS channel and accessible digital broadcast information are naturally recorded in Listen Notes and simply need to guarantee their show. On the off chance that you don't see your show recorded, you can present your digital broadcast using their site or through your Buzz sprout dashboard.

Digital recording Addict

Even though Podcast Addict isn't viewed as a significant registry like Apple Podcasts, it's the most well-known digital broadcast application among Android clients with more than 9,000,000 audience members. Search your show's title to check whether you're now recorded in their information base. If you don't see your digital broadcast, you can submit it to the catalog, and your show will show up in outcomes within 24 hours.

Pod chaser

Pod chaser resembles an intuitive IMDB for digital broadcast makers. Pod chaser's audience members can look for new substance inside the application, and view the webcast's profile page for data about the substance and its makers.

This digital broadcast application is a fantastic method to show your work and interface with fans straightforwardly through its inherent online media components.

Guarantee your maker profile in Pod chaser

Pocket Casts

Pocket Cast's podcasting application (claimed by NPR) includes incredible channels to help manage audience members through an ocean of substance to discover the shows they'll adore.

Pocket Casts is presently free and accessible across iOS, **Android**, Alexa, Car Play, Apple Watch, and considerably more.

Present your web recording to Pocket Casts

Radio Public

Radio Public is a generally utilized application that has been around for more than 15 years. The application focuses on the accomplishment of autonomous makers with hand-curated playlists that exhibit content and a huge load of supportive highlights for podcasters.

Clients can tune in on their work area or cell phone (iOS and Android).

Confirm your web recording on Radio Public

Cast box

Cast box webcast registry began in 2016 to streamline the cycle of web recording disclosure. They've since delivered a few useful assets for discovering content, including an AI-fueled web crawler, and have more than 95 million scenes in their library.

To get recorded in Cast box, pursue a record in their Creator Studio. Select the Claim Ownership tab and furnish them with your email address and RSS connect to finish the interaction.

Make your Creator Studio account

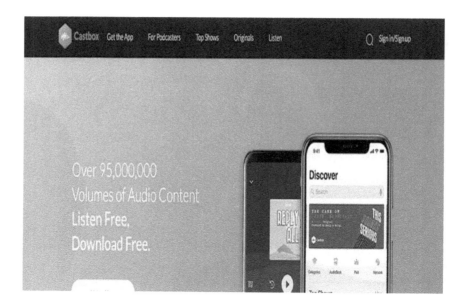

IPodder

IPodder's online catalog highlights hand-picked digital broadcasts across more than 20 classifications, including radio music stations. There's right now no application for the index yet, so audience members need a work area (or an in-telephone program and WiFi) to stream content. When you present your show to the catalog, the group will survey it for endorsement within 48 hours.

Deezer

Deezer's UI is like spottily yet is fundamentally a European application (even though anybody can utilize it). Like spottily, the stage began as a music real-time feature, however now likewise incorporates verbally expressed word sound. Getting your digital broadcast on Deezer gets your show before its 14 million clients, and all the cash produced from advertisements on Deezer goes straightforwardly to supporting craftsmen and podcasters.

Player FM

Player FM is a cloud-synchronized web recording application that focuses on webcast revelation, specialty subjects, and custom-made suggestions. It's an incredible asset for outside the box podcasters and enthusiasts of specialty content.

Add your RSS channel to Player FM

Ladies in Podcasting

Ladies in Podcasting is a catalog only for ladies makers and plans to give an equivalent voice to all makers in the podcasting local area. This catalog is an amazing spot to list your substance on the off chance that you have a show intended for a basically female crowd.

Ladies in Podcasting is at present not tolerating new digital broadcasts, yet return in a couple of months for refreshes from their group!

Present your webcast to Women in Podcasting

Learn Out Loud

Learn out Laud's index generally includes instructive and useful substance and pulls in audience members who need to learn. If you have an instructive digital broadcast (history, writing, science, self-advancement, religion, and so forth), this could be an incredible stage for you! Pursue a Learn Out Loud record to start the accommodation cycle. Present your digital recording to Learn Out Loud More approaches to circulate your digital broadcast Digital broadcast indexes aren't the best way to get your show out there. Investigate these less customary digital broadcast dispersion channels and figure out how to use everyone for your show's potential benefit.

Facebook

Posting short video clasps and audio clips of your show is perhaps the most ideal approach to use Facebook to become your digital recording. You can make visual audio clips with Buzz sprout, and incorporate connect to your web recording site inside your post so watchers can buy into your show!

YouTube

Posting video film of your digital broadcast to YouTube (rather than still-outline cover workmanship) is an incredible method to impart your substance to individuals who may not utilize a podcasting application. You can utilize the stage to communicate with watchers in the remarks segment and distribute reduced down clasps of your substance to create interest in your show. Learn all you require to know before distributing your substance on YouTube and conclude whether it's the correct move for your digital recording.

Sound Cloud

On the off chance that you decide to utilize Sound Cloud to convey your substance, we propose you make a free record. After you have a Sound cloud account, you can transfer your sound documents and connection scenes to your digital broadcast site so clients can buy into your show. We're generally keeping watch for new web recording registries, so don't hesitate to contact us on Twitter, or the remarks beneath, on the off chance that you are aware of any catalogs we missed!

Niche Directories

Specialty Directories

Kathryn Katz of www.webcast1.com has distributed a supportive article in Jill Whalen's staggering High Ranking Advisor regarding the matter of specialty catalogs. This is what she needed to say.

Discovering Free Niche Directories

The estimation of specialty catalogs

As web indexes place increasingly more accentuation on "connect prevalence," site proprietor's end up constrained not exclusively to improve their website, however, to discover other quality sites in their specialty market that will connect to their site. Numerous specialty web indexes like Business.com, IRED.com, and MedMarket.com will list your site, however at a cost. For those site proprietors that are dealing with a strict spending plan, paying for each connection isn't just costly, yet not in their spending plan.

Yet, don't surrender; there are numerous quality, free specialty registries out there. The greatest test is discovering them. Here are three simple strategies to discover free specialty indexes:

Strategy 1: "Web index Search"

Go to your #1 internet searcher (mine is Google), and type when all is said in done keyword(s) identified with your webpage. For instance, if I have a wedding food provider site, I would type in "wedding." Usually, well-positioning specialty registries will put in the Top 10 outcomes. For this situation, WeddingLinksGalore.com is positioned #1 and refers to the portrayal that the registry offers free connections. Navigate to the site and search for an "Add a Link" or "Join Vendor Directory" catch or connection someplace in the route.

Strategy 2: "Registry Search"

Go to a standard index, similar to the Google Directory, and Snap-On "Reference." Click on "Catalogs" and afterward select the significant class that identifies with your site. For instance, if I have a CPA site, I would tap on "Business." At this point, I could decide to present the site to the overall indexes recorded under "Business" like CEOTrak.com or limited my pursuit further to "Bookkeeping Firms" like CPADirectory.com. Likely, I'd wind up experiencing both the "Business" and "Bookkeeping Firms" classes and presenting my site to all free catalogs that were pertinent to my specialty market.

Technique 3: "Rivalry's Links"

Go to your #1 web index and quest for the sites connecting to your rival by composing in link:http://www.competitorswebsite.com. At that point click on each connection and discover indexes that your rival presented their site to. Or on the other hand, go to your rival's site utilizing the Google Toolbar's Page Info > Backward Links highlight. (The Google Toolbar can be downloaded from http://toolbar.google.com/.)

Here's another tip: Don't be hesitant to consider some fresh possibilities while looking for a free specialty index. When searching for a catalog, attempt to think about all business sectors that identify with your site. You'd be astounded at what considers a connected catalog. For instance, I market an overall law practice. I ran over a quality, free specialty catalog, WorkIndex.com that has some expertise in human asset issues. Since the law practice does business and work law, they were qualified for an accommodation to WorkIndex.com under their "Lawful Issues" classification. Remember that you may need to experience a few registries before you locate some quality, free specialty indexes that are ideal for you; notwithstanding, your tirelessness will pay off. You will locate some extraordinary registries that will help your connection prevalence and possibly acquire some quality, directed traffic also.

Best of luck and glad chasing.

Kathryn Katz

Web index Marketing Specialist

Search Marketing – the division of Webcast 1, Inc.

www.webcast1.com

CHAPTER ELEVEN

HOW TO PUBLISH A PODCAST

What is a Podcast Host and how would they work?

Web recording facilitating administrations are organizations that are intended to do precisely what it says on the tin: have your webcast sound documents. This is what that incorporates:

- You transfer your sound to the web recording facilitating site
- They store those sound records
- They gather them all into a web recording 'feed' that individuals can buy in to
- They convey the sound records to your audience members on interest

Presently, there are two different ways to utilize a Podcast facilitating administration.

1. They can have your whole web recording site
2. They can have recently your sound records and you have your site

Choice 1 is exceptionally simple – the host furnishes a site with space for show notes and players that show up consequently. Yet, these destinations will in general be moderately straightforward, and you won't have a lot of control.

Choice 2 takes somewhat more arrangement, however, it gives you way greater adaptability and control. For this situation, you'll be transferring sound records to your host, and afterward distributing the show notes and the sound players on your site. There are a ton of favorable circumstances to this, and the arrangement isn't unreasonably convoluted.

HOW TO UPLOAD A PODCAST

In this article, I will disclose how to transfer a web recording to the web, and make it accessible to your listening public. All things considered, when you make a webcast, you need individuals to hear it, correct?

Yet, transferring and distributing is a stage that foxes virtually every new podcaster. I thoroughly see, as well: it's not instinctive! You don't transfer it to iTunes, Apple Podcasts, Spotify, Google Podcasts, or some other index. You don't transfer it to your site. All things being equal, you transfer your webcast elsewhere totally, and afterward, distribute it to those spots.

Anyway, where for the sake of the small man DO we transfer our webcast records? Where do digital recordings live?

That is the thing that I'm here for – we should discover!

Where You DON'T Upload your Podcast

A great many people are digital broadcast audience members before their podcasters. A couple of years back, before I distributed a solitary webcast scene, I typically discovered shows on iTunes (presently Apple Podcasts). At times I even discovered shows on their sites and tuned in to them there.

So when I began figuring out how to record and blend sound, I made a note that I'd "need to sort out some way to transfer my digital broadcast to iTunes".

I additionally anticipated getting my site and transferring my digital broadcast scenes to that. These two stages, as far as I might be concerned, we're the place where digital recordings lived.

All things considered, on the two fronts, I was a little misguided, because:

- You never transfer digital recording documents to iTunes, or Spotify, or some other catalog
- You never transfer webcast documents to your site

On the subsequent point, it is conceivable, however, here's the reason you shouldn't transfer webcast documents to your website. All things considered, what DO you do? This is what:

- Transfer your webcast documents to a digital broadcast facilitating administration
- Present your whole show to iTunes/Apple Podcast, only a single time
- Distribute scene players, from your host to your site

Digital broadcasts can be a multi-tasked fantasy.

As peruse, you simply can't focus on perusing each blog entry in your feed or staying aware of others via web-based media. In case you're in any way similar to me, you can barely endure a five moment YouTube video without opening another tab.

In an interruption substantial world, numerous individuals are currently going to digital broadcasts. Digital broadcasts are an extraordinary arrangement since we can hear them out while attempting to be beneficial doing different things, such as washing the dishes or driving during our regularly scheduled drive.

While we'd prefer to think we acquire everything a digital recording scene has to bring to the table while tuning in, odds are there's a ton that we miss. This is the reason webcast show notes are a higher priority than any time in recent memory.

Why web recording show notes are significant

For what reason wouldn't you be able to simply record a webcast scene, alter it, and distribute it on iTunes? While it would be decent if the interaction halted there, making an effective web recording is similarly as much about advancement for what it's worth about substance creation.

Web recording show notes are an unquestionable requirement when advertising your digital broadcast. You can consider it the "center point" that gathers all new and what current audience members require to think about every scene. Here are some different reasons why digital recording notes are significant.

Web recording show notes give better detail

At the point when you're tuning in to a digital recording scene, it's so natural to block out and Miss Key focuses. I much of the time do this since I for the most part tune in to webcasts when I'm preparing for the afternoon, having a snappy lunch, or cleaning my condominium.

For individuals like me who are in a surge (which is likely the greater part of your crowd), making web recording show notes allows audience members like us to get up to speed with what we may have missed.

Better SEO with digital broadcast show notes

Much the same as a blog entry, you can add watchwords to your digital broadcast show notes to help the substance's SEO esteem. Your SEO-streamlined webcast title would then turn into your post's feature and the depiction turns into your introduction content.

Make certain to sprinkle a couple of your industry-explicit catchphrases all through your web recording show notes. On the off chance that a catchphrase you as a rule use doesn't apply to the particular scene, forget about it and include different watchwords that are as yet pertinent to your specialty yet in addition to your scene theme. You may simply take advantage of another augmentation of your crowd that way!

Digital broadcast show notes make another piece of valuable content

At the point when you begin delivering digital broadcast scenes routinely, figuring out how to blog will get somewhat harder. Fortunately, webcast show notes can go about as another piece of blog-like substance for your site. You get a considerable lot of the advantages of contributing to a blog, yet you additionally get to repurpose the web recording scene so you're not copying work.

You can likewise divert topics from the digital broadcast show notes into different blog entries.

Star tip: Don't neglect to interface back to each blog entry when you do. It'll support your area authority which assists with your SEO.

Digital broadcast show notes become a center point for your most significant assets

Everybody likes to understand what others are perusing, watching, and tuning in to, yet it gets overpowering to address these inquiries again and again.

At the point when you make a digital broadcast, you get the opportunity to normally raise your number one asset in the discussion and afterward connect to them in your show notes. You can likewise incorporate associate connections which can create some pleasant side pay. Remember to refer to your items and administrations as well!

What to remember for your digital recording show notes

Since you're persuaded digital recording show notes merit a couple of additional means, how about we dive into what goes into a decent webcast synopsis. Something to be thankful for to recollect is that the digital recording content has just done the vast majority of the work for you!

Here are the means by which to pull out the extra data you'll have to make better digital recording show notes:

Most effective method to boost your webcast show notes in 5 simple advances

How to maximize your podcast show notes in 5 easy steps

STEP 1

Write a loose content outline before recording

STEP 2

Have your guests help you with the work

STEP 3

Translate main ideas > transcribing

STEP 4

Share the podcast show notes on social media

STEP 5

Offer bonus content in your podcast show notes

You currently have an overall work process for what to remember for your digital recording show notes. Presently we can begin discussing how to benefit from your webcast show notes. As you most likely are aware, show notes set aside some effort to assemble so these tips will help you preserve energy all the while.

Stage 1: Write a free substance plot before recording

In case you're a little anxious about chronicling your first webcast scenes, don't stress. It's entirely expected to feel that route with anything new. Fortunately, there are a few things you can plan early to quiet your nerves before the meeting. One is to make a rundown of your principal arguments.

Not exclusively does a substance plot assist you with getting sorted out your musings, it will likewise assist you with characterizing what the primary concerns of your digital recording rundown will be. This layout can control the discussion and go about as a guide in assessing your meeting.

Stage 2: Have your visitors help you with the work

Presently, this doesn't mean you'll request that your visitors alter their scenes that wouldn't be acceptable. All things being equal, you can request that they send over any arguments they need to talk about in the scene. At that point, you can utilize those as primary concerns in the web recording synopsis.

You can likewise request that they send over their headshot, bio, and some other data you need before recording the scene so it's all set.

Stage 3: Translate principle thoughts > deciphering

You may have seen that some digital recording has remembered a full scene record for their show notes. While that can be useful for a few, the vast majority simply need the primary concerns on the off chance that they're not going to tune in to the scene. Fundamentally, don't stress over composing each expression of the webcast.

Stage 4: Share the webcast show notes via online media

Your digital broadcast show notes are exceptional bits of substance simply like a blog entry or YouTube video. That implies they're worth sharing and advancing via online media.

You can do this all through the principal seven day stretch of the web recording scene's distribution date and sprinkle it into your online media schedule for future advancement. Because the scene is in your chronicle doesn't mean it's any less deserving of being advanced. Make a point to add social offer catches to your webcast show notes, as well.

To make it a stride further, you can make a Click to Tweet connect for every one of the statements or transform the statements into pin-commendable designs. You could even share the statement designs on Instagram or incorporate the content statement in your inscription. Repurposing content you've just made encourages you to work more brilliant rather than harder.

Stage 5: Offer reward content in your digital broadcast show notes

Who doesn't cherish a decent gift? At the point when you add reward free substance in your digital broadcast show takes note of, a first-time guest might be intrigued enough to join and look at your webcast.

On the off chance that you notice the reward content inside the scene, you may acquire some extra endorsers from the individuals who tune in. On the off chance that building your email list is one of your all-encompassing promoting objectives, this is an extraordinary method to do it.

CHAPTER TWELVE

PROMOTION TIPS FOR YOUR PODCAST

Instructions to advance a digital broadcast:

Much obliged to individuals and brands who have been liberal to share their podcasting tips on the web. The absolute best counsel I discovered dated right back to 2012, which shows exactly how long a few people have been dominating the digital broadcast game. I'll connect to some most loved assets toward the finish of this article too.

Here's the large rundown of digital recording advancement techniques *we're quick to attempt.*

1. Influence your visitor's crowd

Make it simple for visitors to share by making pieces and statement pictures

- We're blessed that our digital broadcast has a meeting design, where we will converse with astounding individuals like Rand Fishing of Mos. and Meghan Kearney Anderson of Hub Spot.
- These individuals have enormous crowds.
- Rand has more than 335,000 Twitter supporters.
- Hub Spot has more than 1 million Facebook fans.

What we'd love to do is make it simple for our visitors to share and advance their digital recording scene. One thought is to send them a note on the day their webcast goes live and incorporate a progression of shareable media:

- Pull quotes
- Pictures
- Connections
- Prewritten tweets and announcements
- Here's an illustration of one of the pictures we made for Meghan's scene:
- Meghan Keaney Anderson quote - get recruited via web-based media
- Here is the email we sent for Rand's first scene (don't hesitate to duplicate it on the off chance that you'd like):
- outreach-email-for-digital broadcast visitors

From this string on Growth Hackers, there's some fascinating counsel to treat digital broadcast advancement like you would content advancement, a zone wherein we have somewhat more experience. Here are the points of interest from the Growth Hackers string:

- Quality > Quantity
- Take care of an issue
- Give noteworthy knowledge
- Hustle similarly as to make
- Influence your visitor's crowd
- ^^ It's this last one that we're eager to try different things within some pleasant manners.

2. Advance via web-based media ... in twelve unique manners

Offer rich media, short clips, video, pictures, mysteries, evergreen — anything you can consider

We're so fortunate to have the stunning informal organizations that we do. There's simply such a lot of innovativeness and enjoyment to be had with advancing a digital recording via web-based media.

First off, share an update when the scene initially goes live.

At that point, continue to share.

Here are a few thoughts:

> Pin your scene tweet or Facebook post, including the iTunes URL.

> Create quote pictures in Canva or Pablo. Offer these as independent social updates with a connection to iTunes.

Here's the Canva format that we're utilizing.

> Create 15-second audio clip cuts. Transfer to Soundcloud. At that point share on Twitter.

Twitter has a truly perfect usage of Soundcloud sound explicitly. Individuals can play the sound right from their Twitter stream. tweet-with-SoundCloud-implant

> Tease the following scene 24 hours early.

> Reshare the web recording scene on different occasions.

We do 3x to Twitter the primary day, 2x to Facebook the main week.

> Talk about the in the background stuff in an Instagram story. —

3. Delivery at any rate 3 scenes on the dispatch day

"I got antagonistic audits from individuals who had tuned in to the primary scene and were vexed that there was just one."

- The above statement is from Pat Flynn, the originator of Smart Passive Income. His recommendation about the dispatch amount is directly by the best tips from others, as well.
- Distribute 3 to 5 scenes when you first dispatch.
- From our exploration, the base number of scenes to have at dispatch is three. When all is said in done, more is always

better. We had seven meetings complete before we dispatched our digital broadcast, with three scenes getting ready for dispatch day and two each for the accompanying fourteen days.

- This multi-dispatch system is a critical part of Jason Zook's arrangement for hitting the New and Noteworthy segment of iTunes, which, as we referenced above, is a gigantic method to get traffic.
- Jason's arrangement relies on these two ideas:
- Record and delivery a few digital broadcasts on dispatch day (3-5)
- Assemble your crowd before dispatching if conceivable

4. Convert the sound to a YouTube video

Name your video "Meeting with ... " for possible SEO

One thing we'd love to have the option to do with the webcast is to repurpose it from multiple points of view as could be expected. A few organizations do slick things, blending live video (on Facebook and Periscope) with the live web recording meeting. We're eager to attempt a marginally unique course.

We're quick to add each scene of the digital recording to our YouTube channel.

With a YouTube adaptation, you get a small bunch of advantages:

- Video to share via web-based media
- Shut subtitling and records consequently from YouTube (extraordinary for availability in case you're not going to decipher)
- Web optimization benefits
- This last one is truly energizing.

BROUGHT TO YOU BY

Attempt our full heap of brand building apparatuses

We've constructed a full heap of online media instruments to assist current brands with developing their mindfulness, commitment, and deals.

- Start a free 14-day preliminary
- At times, Google esteems video 53x as much as the text.
- So while we're confident that our show notes help us rank a piece for long-tail terms in Google, we're additionally energized that having a YouTube variant could support our rankings also.
- Scott Britton utilized this procedure to great impact with his meeting webcast, picking a particular methodology of positioning for "[Guest Name] Interview." So for us, this may resemble:
- Rand Fishkin meet
- Meeting with Rand Fishkin
- By adding this to the YouTube title, fingers-crossed, we'll see some great outcomes!
- To change over sound (.mp3 for example) to video (.mov), you can utilize a wide range of instruments. Google's help place suggests iMovie for Mac clients and Windows Live Movie Maker for PC clients. I immediately bounced into Screenflow to assemble a quick video form of our digital broadcast.
- Pick a material of 2,560 pixels wide by 1,440 pixels tall for the best survey at 2K goal (there are a modest bunch of other ideal measurements here in case you're not intrigued by 2K)
- Get free stock video film from Videvo or Pexels. Circling video is ideal; search "circle."

Incorporate a brisk thumbnail both of your show's logo or your visitor (or both). In case you're feeling particularly proactive, you can clarify the video with connections, cards, and more from inside the YouTube maker studio

5. Present your webcast to pod catchers and aggregators

Pod catchers — a beautiful cool name, correct? — are essentially applications that play web recordings. The most well-known one is the primary digital broadcast application in iOS; it's the one with the purple symbol and an image of a mouthpiece. Past the iOS pod catcher, many other applications gather and play web recordings, and there are a large group of sites that highlight new webcasts and help with disclosure.

Here's a snappy rundown of 10 of the more well-known ones:

- Cloudy
- Stitcher
- Digital broadcast Addict
- Digital broadcast subedit
- Podcast Land (your digital broadcast is consequently recorded here if it's in iTunes)
- Tune In
- Bello Collective
- Castro
- Digital broadcast Republic
- Unhappy

Podcast Land has an included web recording of the month, which is picked by client votes.

(As a rule, your digital recording will work extraordinary with any of these administrations, especially in case you're now on iTunes. The smartest choice is attempting each application out for yourself to guarantee a smooth encounter for your audience members.)

6. Interpret the sound

Attempt assistance like Rev.com ($1/minute) or Fiverr ($5)

A great deal of profoundly effective webcasts offers a full record of the whole show. We're deciding to take a somewhat extraordinary course with this, pulling out featured bits of the record and remembering these for the show notes. Would you rather have the full record? Or then again chose extracts?

The record is incredible for SEO benefits and as a spot to gather drives (you can add lead catch structures and connections to your show notes page). We desire to catch a portion of these advantages still while setting aside time and cash from doing the full record.

7. Set up a fourteen-day evaluations party

Quite possibly the main variables in driving a web recording up the graphs in iTunes (and into the New and Noteworthy segment) is the rate at which you gather downloads and positive surveys in a little while. You have two months from when your digital recording dispatches to get to New and Noteworthy. The initial fourteen days of these are particularly significant.

Here is a couple of gathering arranging segments that can help make these a little while after the web recording dispatch feels like an occasion:

- Run giveaways (more on this underneath)
- Arrange a genuine gathering on dispatch day, either face to face or using Facebook Live
- Distribute fourteen days of digital recording themed blog content. This post is a model!
- Change out the email marks on your email and in your group's help messages

- Get your partners and friends executives to post and tweet about it
- Email 10 companions each day

8. Run a giveaway challenge

Step by step instructions to enter: Leave an audit on iTunes

The appeal of free stuff and limits can be an amazing spark to get more tunes in to your web recording. Also, here's the cherry on top: Ask for an audit on iTunes as a feature of the section prerequisites for your giveaway. This will ideally acquire you more audits, which will help the social confirmation on your digital recording and get iTunes to pay heed.

If you have the spending plan to take into consideration, these might make some extraordinary giveaways:

- Shirts
- Item limits
- Stickers

What's more, on the off chance that you don't exactly have the financial plan:

- Notice in the show notes
- A holler toward the finish of the show
- A 5-minute visitor spot on the web recording

The most ideal approach to this is to just commence the challenge either via web-based media or by referencing it on the show. Request that individuals leave an iTunes survey to enter.

One of the interesting things about this is the way to connect with somebody who leaves an audit. There's no clear method to do it, however fortunately most usernames now are a nearby enough guess of another person's online media handle that you resemble

The Overlooked Podcast Growth Lever: SEO

Website optimization endeavors on digital recordings are regularly ignored and belittled, so use this agenda to ensure that your digital recording is completely enhanced!

- Pick a watchword for every scene
- Ensure you're adding your objective watchword in the URL, title tag, and meta depiction
- Make a page/blog entry for every scene
- Compose an introduction with 2-3 rundown list items
- Supplement a picture
- Connection to significant item or arrangement page
- Decipher the web recording beneath the inserted media player
- Add a source of inspiration (CTA) to an important landing page or structure
- Get social and advance your web recording (and inquire your companions, family, and associates to share it to their informal communities, as well!

(Make certain to scratch everything off the rundown before pushing ahead!)

You're Guide to Podcast Directories

Since you've characterized your intended interest group – as well as get a handle on why they're tuning in to webcasts – you'll need to publicize and construct your crowd. On the off chance that you run your own webcast, there are several online indexes you ought to consider presenting your show to:

- ITunes, which makes up 75% of the worldwide advanced music market, is an extraordinary approach to share digital recordings. To build your odds of getting your digital recording endorsed, follow the tips laid out on their webcast specs page, counting these principle prerequisites:

- Watchers should have the option to get to the substance without entering a secret phrase.
- It should meet the RSS 2.0 detail.
- You ought to incorporate the suggested iTunes RSS labels.
- Utilize fitting labels in the titles and depiction because the iTunes web index utilizes these labels to help clients find important digital broadcasts.
- You should set the <explicit> labels to "yes" on the off chance that you plan on utilizing any profane language in your webcast. Remember that you can't utilize express language in your title, depiction, or cover workmanship, regardless of whether you utilize this tag.
- You can't utilize any pictures that praise sex, medications, viciousness, or other content that might be deciphered as disgusting.

You are precluded from utilizing reserved words or pictures without earlier approval from the brand name holders.

CONCLUSION

In this way, you have taken in a ton about Podcasting. You should understand what a Podcast is, the way you can make a powerful Podcast, a few uses for Podcasting, and you should feel good utilizing this innovation on the PC on the off chance that you ever expected to do it again. Ponder internally: "Do I want Podcasting? Is there a future use I may anticipate? Notwithstanding recording my own, strength I use them more for tuning in and keeping up on news and amusement?"

Test with Podcasting and have a great time doing thusly! They don't need to be hour-long accounts. More often than not, they are more viable when kept more limited and when the speed is consistent (not sluggish). This assists in withholding your crowd's consideration.

With the increment of simple to-utilize programs and the expansion of versatile innovation, we can make, access, and tune in to digital recordings any place we go. There is an immense choice of web recordings being offered to purchasers, with new ones being offered regularly. Regardless of what subject you are keen on, odds are there is a digital broadcast for it. Still no? Why not make your own!

Webcasts offer instructors and understudies better approaches to share information and impart about understandings. I trust that this learning object has expanded your comprehension of podcasting and has permitted you to think about utilizing them in your life.

Ideally, you don't feel scared by this point if this is the first occasion when you have truly investigated Podcasts and Podcasting. If you're not certain about expecting to record them yourself at this moment, recall there are a lot of Podcasts out there on the internet that you can download and tune in to, either at your work area, on your versatile MP3 player, or even copied to CDs for use in the vehicle. Appreciate! Cast-on!

www.ingramcontent.com/pod-product-compliance
Lightning Source LLC
Chambersburg PA
CBHW031238050326
40690CB00007B/860